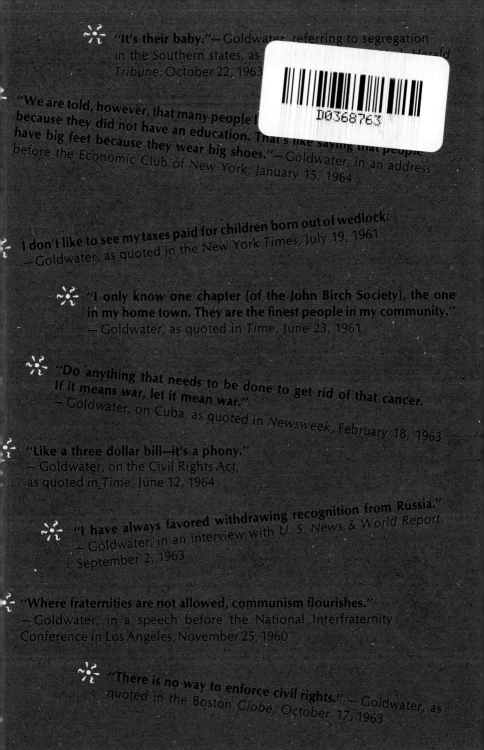

"It's their baby."—Goldwater, referring to segregation in the Southern states, as ~~quoted in the~~ Herald Tribune, October 22, 1963

"We are told, however, that many people f___ because they did not have an education. That's like saying that people have big feet because they wear big shoes."—Goldwater, in an address before the Economic Club of New York, January 15, 1964

I don't like to see my taxes paid for children born out of wedlock. —Goldwater, as quoted in the New York Times, July 19, 1961

"I only know one chapter [of the John Birch Society], the one in my home town. They are the finest people in my community." — Goldwater, as quoted in Time, June 23, 1961

"Do anything that needs to be done to get rid of that cancer. If it means war, let it mean war." — Goldwater, on Cuba, as quoted in Newsweek, February 18, 1963

"Like a three dollar bill—it's a phony." — Goldwater, on the Civil Rights Act, as quoted in Time, June 12, 1964

"I have always favored withdrawing recognition from Russia." — Goldwater, in an interview with U. S. News & World Report, September 2, 1963

"Where fraternities are not allowed, communism flourishes." — Goldwater, in a speech before the National Interfraternity Conference in Los Angeles, November 25, 1960

"There is no way to enforce civil rights." — Goldwater, as quoted in the Boston Globe, October 17, 1963

THE GOLDWATER CAPER

Books by Richard H. Rovere

Howe and Hummel: Their True and Scandalous History

The General and the President (*with Arthur M. Schlesinger, Jr.*)

Affairs of State: The Eisenhower Years

Senator Joe McCarthy

The American Establishment and Other Reports,
Opinions, and Speculations

RICHARD H. ROVERE

The Goldwater Caper

With cartoons by Bill Mauldin

 HARCOURT, BRACE & WORLD, INC.

NEW YORK

for Betsy

PREFACE

Back in another age—that is to say, a year and a half ago, in
the autumn of 1963—I started what was to be a short book on
Barry Goldwater. I was writing about him on November 22,
when my son phoned and told me that President Kennedy had
just been shot in Dallas.

I abandoned the project that day and had no expectation of
reviving it. For one thing, I was suddenly no longer much interested in Barry Goldwater. For another, I felt that he was finished in American politics. My lack of acumen was evidently
matched by his. But by spring, I found myself writing about
him again, as he found himself running again, and shortly before November 3, 1964, I decided to do a postelection book.
I thought of it as a kind of souvenir volume, and my rationale
was provided by Walter Lippmann, who, a couple of days after
the returns were in, said that he had the delicious feeling of a
man who had just got over a very bad toothache. I recalled at
the time the delight with which my children used to keep and
treasure their baby teeth after they fell or were pulled out. It
is, apparently, a human failing to collect mementoes of misery
as well as of pleasure. I offer this book as a souvenir of a toothache.

A word is necessary about the dating of the pieces in Part
One. I have dated the first two chapters November 22, 1963
because that is the last day on which I worked on them. They
were to be part of the book I put aside when I learned the news
of that black Friday. A small part of their content had appeared

in the *New Yorker* for November 2, 1963, but most of it has not before been published. The better part of the third chapter was also part of the first project, but nearly all of it was published in *Harper's Magazine* for September 1964.

The eighth chapter was commissioned by *Encounter,* a London publication, and appeared in the October 1964 edition. The twelfth appears in this book for the first time. The other chapters were published in the *New Yorker*; some I have cut, some I have amplified, some I have republished without change. In every case, they bear the date of submission. My obligation to the *New Yorker* is large not only for its commissioning of those reports that have appeared in its pages but for making it possible for me, over the past twenty-one years, to keep a close watch on politics in general. Elsewhere in this volume I poke a certain amount of fun at Goldwater for his list of those who have provided him with literary "crutches." A bit of the joke is now on me. I do not think of William Shawn and Gardner Botsford, of the *New Yorker,* as crutch-dispensers, but if I am able to walk alone, it is largely thanks to their counsel and instruction. John Fischer, of *Harper's,* and Melvin J. Lasky, of *Encounter,* have also offered encouragement and support. And I must salute several of my friends and colleagues: Peter Lisagor, Robert J. Donovan, Mary McGrory, Murray Kempton, Charles Mohr, Page Wilson, Mary Moore Molony, Arthur Schlesinger, Jr., Rowland Evans, Robert Novak, and Joseph Alsop. And there must be a special word of thanks for one who may be uneasy in this company—Victor Gold, Senator Goldwater's assistant press secretary, who provided courtesy, jokes, creature comforts, and illumination on an extraordinary tour of the South reported upon at some length in the pages that follow. I could not have made it through or up to 1964 without the unwarranted sympathy and aid of Eleanor Burgess Rovere.

R.H.R.

New York
January, 1965

CONTENTS

Contents

x

PART ONE

Some Views of Goldwater and Goldwaterism

The conservative movement found Senator Goldwater, Senator Goldwater found the movement; it was like the meeting of the Blue and the White Nile.

—William Rusher, publisher of the *National Review*, quoted in *Partisan Review*, Fall 1964

I know Barry fairly well. He is a great American. . . . I raised around two-thousand dollars in my state and sent it to him early in 1958. . . . Barry Goldwater has political know-how and the painstaking genius to use the know-how with regard to infinite details. He is a superb political organizer, and inspires deep and lasting loyalty. He is absolutely superb in his Americanism, has the political and moral courage to stand by his Americanist principles, and in my opinion can be trusted to stand by them until hell freezes over. I'd love to see him President of the United States, and maybe one day we shall.

—Robert Welch, the "Founder" of the John Birch Society, in *The Blue Book*, 1958

My friends, I am persuaded that there is a destiny in the affairs of men and of nations. There are moments of history when power is given to a man to do what is right for his fellow men, when Divine Providence intervenes that God's plan for His creation may be carried out. Mr. Chairman, I place in nomination for the office of President of the United States a man with the courage of heroes, United States Senator Barry Goldwater of Arizona.

—Governor Paul Fannin, of Arizona, to the 1960 Republican National Convention at Chicago

BE THE FIRST IN YOUR PRECINCT TO OWN
A BARRY GOLDWATER SWEATSHIRT

You'll delight in watching liberals recoil in terror when they see you in your BARRY GOLDWATER SWEATSHIRT. You'll find your BGSS imbues you with renewed courage to suffer the slings and arrows of the extremist lunatic fringe of the ultra left.

The Barry Goldwater sweatshirt displays a nearly life-sized head of Barry Goldwater, with his name below to identify him to uninitiated liberals.

—From an advertisement in the *National Review*, July 17, 1962. The BGSS sold at $3.95 and was distributed by the Conservative Book Store, 228 Massachusetts Avenue, Indianapolis, Indiana.

✳ THE CHEERFUL MALCONTENT: A LETTER FROM WASHINGTON

November 22, 1963

Senator Goldwater appeared before the Republican Platform Committee in Chicago on July 19, 1960 and proposed that it cease its labors. The day of the "platform" was over, he told the committee, which sat in the Crystal Room of the Blackstone Hotel. What the age demanded, he explained, was the replacement of the "platform" by a "declaration of principles." Lexicographers, by and large, hold that a "declaration of principles" is what a platform is, or ought to be, but Goldwater is no respecter of lexicographers. "The American people have become cynically suspicious of platforms," he told the committee. "Principles," on the other hand, continue to be highly regarded. "I suggest," he said, "that the American people will be far more eager to place their destiny in the hands of a man who announces his beliefs and principles than in the hands of a man who promises and promises and promises and promises, knowing that he cannot keep his promises."

Goldwater proved a constructive critic. He had something of his own to offer. He submitted to the Platform Committee, meeting on the eve of the convention that was to nominate Richard M. Nixon and Henry Cabot Lodge, a document drawn up in his office and entitled "Suggested Declaration of Principles." It ran to about a thousand words of what might be called Classical, or Mandarin, Platformese:

We condemn deficit financing. . . . We must proclaim for Victory in the Cold War. . . . We denounce and condemn those [who] lead us to piecemeal surrender. . . . We believe that every man is entitled to an equal position on the starting line in the race for personal achievement. . . . We deplore the trend to thrust all responsibility on the federal bureaucracy. . . . We proclaim . . . We condemn . . . We offer . . . In this regard, we recognize . . . We denounce and condemn . . . We affirm . . . We denounce . . . We condemn . . . We deplore. . . .

It looked like a platform and sounded like a platform, and it seemed, in its proud negativism and its even-handed denunciation, a really swinging platform for a candidate who had announced, as Goldwater had, in *The Conscience of a Conservative,* then hot off the presses and high on the best-seller lists, that "My aim is not to pass laws but to repeal them." But it takes a law to repeal a law, and Goldwater's "Suggested Principles" singled out no laws for repeal.

The Platform Committee heard Goldwater out and then got down to the trying business of putting together a platform. The draftsmen, working under the chairmanship of Charles H. Percy, a Republican businessman eager for a political career,* proceeded on the assumption that their mission was to produce a platform for Richard M. Nixon. The mission was completed. A Nixon platform was drafted—several degrees to the left of Barry Goldwater, several to the right of Nelson Rockefeller, fuzzy and flaky on some issues, bold on others, and defensive, naturally, about the Eisenhower administration, which Goldwater once called a "dime-store New Deal."

Just as everything in Chicago seemed in order, there was a roar of outrage in New York. Nelson Rockefeller was greatly annoyed. He wasn't sure he could support the ticket. The plat-

---

* In 1964, he ran for governor of Illinois and for a time seemed headed for victory. Had he won the office, he would have been among those seriously considered for the Presidential nomination in 1968. He supported Goldwater but in an almost inaudible voice. He is still a businessman. The incumbent Democrat, Otto Kerner, won.

form, he felt, was defective in several respects—not far-reaching enough in its civil-rights proposals, a bit weaseling in its pledges to promote economic growth, not firm enough in its commitment to certain increases in military power. Appalled by the prospect of running without Rockefeller's unqualified support, Nixon flew to New York, and in the Governor's apartment negotiated an agreement that was to be known to the Chicago convention as the Treaty of Fifth Avenue. Several wires were opened to Chicago, and Nixon had the platform redrafted in such a way as to make it more acceptable to Governor Rockefeller, which meant, of course, that it was less acceptable to President Eisenhower and downright distasteful to Senator Goldwater. Actually, the changes were not in themselves numerous or important enough to detain historians for very long. It was not the revisions themselves that were significant, but the fact that they were made to appease Rockefeller. In any case, Goldwater called their acceptance "a surrender . . . the Munich of the Republican Party." The convention adopted the platform without discussion or amendment.

Goldwater, for his part, adjusted quickly. His own 1960 boom hadn't given him even a crack at the Vice-Presidential nomination, and he was at once magnanimous and threatening in defeat. Exhorting his followers to get out and work for the candidate who had accepted the "Munich," he said, "The great Republican Party is our historical house. This is our home. Now some of us don't agree with every statement in the official platform . . . but I might remind you that this is true of every platform. . . ." (As he was later to say, "At their best, political platforms are packets of lies.") He also said, "Let's grow up, conservatives. We want to take this party back, and I think some day we can." Still and all, the whole affair hardened him in his dislike of platforms. He continues to favor their replacement by a "declaration of principles." It appears, though, that he now approaches the matter in a somewhat different way. In 1960, he maintained that a man is known by the principles he keeps. "If you will tell me what a man believes," he told the Platform

Committee in Chicago, "I can predict with reasonable accuracy how this man will respond in any given situation." More recently, he has been defending his proposal on the ground that the whole virtue of promulgating such a declaration of principles is that it would absolutely defy accurate prediction. In the course of an interview published in *U. S. News & World Report* on October 22, 1962, he was asked if he still favored his 1960 position; he said he did, and explained the advantages of it as follows:

Instead of so many words, as might be found in a political platform, say we included a statement like "We believe in the freedom of the individual." All right, Senator Javits can take that in New York and apply it to civil rights, the Negro question, everything else. I can take it and apply it to "right to work." I can apply it to states' rights.

This observation alone should guarantee Goldwater a place in the history of American *Realpolitik*. It puts him, as an elucidator, alongside the late George Washington Plunkitt, a man who put generations of Tammany Hall leaders in his debt by making clear the moral distinctions between "dishonest graft" and "honest graft." * On civil rights, the differences between Goldwater and Javits are, if anything, larger than the differences between Goldwater, say, and Robert Kennedy. Javits repeatedly criticizes the administration on the ground that its proposals are inadequate. He would go much further. Goldwater would go nowhere near so far. Javits has no use for the states'-rights argument. Goldwater speaks of states' rights as though their omission from the Ten Commandments were a mere oversight on God's part. And indeed it is hard to find anything at all—anything likely to be at issue in American politics in the period

* Another notable contribution, in spirit more like Goldwater's, was once made by Henry Agard Wallace, Vice-President of the United States in Franklin D. Roosevelt's second term. Asked why, in a talk about the "general welfare," he had been rather unclear as to what he meant by the term, Wallace got straight to the heart of the matter by saying, "I believe that in a democracy every individual ought to define the general welfare in his own way."

ahead—on which Goldwater and Javits could agree, except, of course, a "principle"—such as "the freedom of the individual." The remarkable thing about Goldwater's explanation of how he and Senator Javits might find a way of living together was the fact that he made it—that he spelled it out. He didn't shrink at going on record as taking both the highest and the lowest view of a moral value. Politicians all along have understood the role of "principle" in practical politics.* It encourages symbiosis—the cohabitation in one environment of creatures as different in their political conformation, coloration, and feeding habits as Goldwater and Javits. But the delicious ambiguity of the term is discussed guardedly and of course ambiguously. ("Our differences are policies, our agreements principles," President McKinley, one of the masters, once explained, explaining, naturally, nothing.) Goldwater explained the value of ambiguity in unambiguous, concrete terms.

Something in Goldwater—it may be artlessness, it may be artfulness—leads him to expose and explain every little sham, every bit of political humbug he perpetrates. For example, one practical difficulty the Senator faces is that his Senate term expires in 1964. If he decides to run for the Presidency rather than the Senate, he will risk having no office at all in 1965. It is always difficult to arrange for a political future when one has no political present. Goldwater could, of course, run for both offices in 1964. There is no federal law against it, and he has been assured by the Attorney General of Arizona that he would violate no state law if he were a candidate for both the Senate and the Presidency. There would be a certain awkwardness in this, however, for in 1960, Goldwater went all over the South denouncing Lyndon Johnson for seeking the Vice-Presidency

---

* So have statesmen, and even philosophers. "Don't tell me we agree in principle," General George Catlett Marshall once said impatiently, toward the end of a conference. "That just means we don't agree on anything." And John Stuart Mill: "[The] principles which men profess on any controverted subject are usually a very incomplete exponent of the opinions they really hold."

and a Senate seat at the same time. (The Texas legislature had rewritten Texas law in order to enable Johnson to do this.) In speech after speech, Goldwater called Johnson "the slickest political trickster of our time" and charged him with a "lack of courage to stand up and fight for one office at a time." His righteous indignation now stands in the way of a simple exercise of prudence. In August 1963, Stewart Alsop, of the *Saturday Evening Post,* asked him if he intended to accept the opinion of his state's counsel. He replied: "No, I can't do that after what I said about Lyndon in 1960—they'd run me out of the country. But if I hadn't opened my big mouth so loud, I might do it."

"I wish that not only no act of mine but no thought of mine should be unknown," Thomas Jefferson wrote in the last year of his Presidency. Goldwater seems to feel the same way, or somewhat the same way. He sometimes goes beyond Jefferson. He dissembles and explains that he is dissembling. There was a certain vanity in Jefferson's candor. There appears to be none, or very little, in Goldwater's. Jefferson must have felt, as he had every right to feel, that the workings of his mind were interesting and important and relevant. Goldwater's leads him to tell Alsop, "You know, I haven't really got a first-class brain" and to cite a domestic colloquy with Mrs. Goldwater after Mr. Goldwater had read to her "and a couple of her girl friends" a speech he planned shortly to deliver. He observed that the trio seemed unmoved, and "So I said, what the hell is the matter, and Peggy said, look, this is a sophisticated audience, they're not a lot of lame-brains like you, they don't spend their time looking at TV Westerns. You can't give them that corn."

Jefferson called the Presidency a "splendid misery." Goldwater, asked by Alsop how he feels as he faces the possibility that he may, within a matter of months, find himself in the White House, said, "Frankly, it scares the hell out of me." This is an unsettling admission when it comes from a man who insists that the United States "take the offensive in dealing with the worldwide Communist threat" and who, discussing the risks of thermonuclear war, has said, "If possible, overt hostilities should always be avoided." This display of strategic *sang-froid* is to be found in Goldwater's *Why Not Victory?*, published in 1962. It could be that what scares the hell out of Goldwater is the prospect of assuming the Presidency after having said these things. On the other hand, he has since—in October 1963, in a speech before the Military Order of the World Wars—admitted to another dread. Addressing himself to the current situation in the Pentagon, he said, "I say, fear the civilians—they're taking over." He goes on and on. To *Newsweek* he says, regarding his own plans, "If I thought I'd get my tail whipped badly, I'd say the hell with it." "I know nothing about farming," he says, and goes on to call for "a prompt and final termination of all farm subsidies."

It is all, one is told, part of the Senator's relaxed style. He is, by his own acknowledgment,* a bit on the loose-lipped side, and he says it all straight out, and he is also a smiler, ready to be pardners with any straight-shooting, straight-talking man like Jacob Javits. The style blends oddly with his conservatism. The hard-sell copy for one of the several authorized Goldwater biographies (*Barry Goldwater,* by Rob Wood and Dean Smith) says, "There's no escaping it! Barry Goldwater is like no other Conservative who ever lived." There may be *some* escaping it. There were probably Conservatives like Goldwater in Cleon's Athens. But he is, in our American setting, different. The last conservative leader of standing, Robert A. Taft, was a prickly, stiff-necked man who had what one of his political managers once despairingly called "an unmarketable personality." Taft combined prickliness with starchiness. He had the look of a banker who might foreclose the mortgage tomorrow morning. He had the manner of a knuckle-rapping schoolmaster. One

---

* Even when his "hip-shooting" was a big issue in 1964, he could say to Hermann Schreiber, of *Der Spiegel:* "Now I'll have to admit that I possibly do shoot from the hip." He amplified: "I've been exposed to problems and I don't have to stop and think in details about them."

look at him and it was plain that he was a Republican of the most conservative stripe. Taft was square, in his generation's sense of the word and ours.

Goldwater is something else altogether. His personality is by far the most marketable of his assets. He is handsome, good-natured, gallant, athletic, and full of redeeming surprises. He is a cheerful malcontent, a flexible standpatter. He is without vanity, and this is attractive in any man. Yet he has taken it upon himself to play a role that seems to call for a great deal of vanity. He is, if we are to take him at his word, a reformer. He is a critic of ideas. He has not thus far offered himself as a superior organizer or administrator. His differences with the Eisenhower and Kennedy administrations have not been over the way certain things were done, but over the fact that they were being done at all. ("I have little interest in streamlining government or in making it more efficient, for I mean to reduce its size.") He perceives, he keeps telling us, fundamental errors not merely in our political institutions, but also in the basic assumptions about the nature of man and life and society on which the foreign and domestic policies of the last four Presidents have been based. "The root difference," he says, in *The Conscience of a Conservative,* "between the Conservatives and the Liberals of today is that the Conservatives take account of the *whole* man, while the Liberals tend to look only at the material side of man's nature." This is one of those sentences that can be turned upside down and inside out and hind end foremost without making any less sense or any more, but one would be obtuse indeed to claim ignorance as to what he is driving at. His opponents, most of them, think that society, through the instrumentality of government, should render special aid to the materially disadvantaged. In the common interest, according to the view he opposes, governments should use their powers to raise the levels of education, health, and material well-being; there is nothing wrong—on the contrary, there is something good—about steadily broadening concepts of the general welfare. Now these ideas and others with which they are associated are not peculiar to the United States

"AW, COME ON BACK—I WAS ONLY KIDDING."

"Sometimes I think this country would be better off if we could just saw off the Eastern Seaboard and let it float out to sea."

—Goldwater, as quoted in the Chicago *Tribune,* September 30, 1961

or to the past few decades. Almost since the onset of the industrial revolution, they have permeated Western thinking on the nature of the good society—the good *industrial* society—and they have been an enormous shaping force in most of the Western world throughout this century and part of the one before it. Goldwater holds them to be dead wrong, to be contrary to the "ancient and tested truths" whose primacy he would restore. "Throughout history," he announces, "true Conservatism has been at war equally with autocrats and with 'democratic' Jacobins."

It is not clear who besides Goldwater has ever spoken for "true Conservatism," but it is clear that if he is serious about these things (and that, one must concede, is possible, despite his apparent lack of seriousness about other things) he has set himself a task that calls for labors of the intellect and spirit comparable in magnitude and rigor to those undertaken by Jefferson, or by Martin Luther, or—perhaps the only time there will ever be such a bracketing—by Lenin. It is a task that calls not only for vanity and arrogance, but also for passion and a kind of heroic self-confidence. Yet Goldwater, in the midst of telling everyone what must be done, constantly calls attention to what he regards as his own inadequate qualifications not alone for leadership, but for simple analysis. He characterizes his own mind as weak and his spirit as unwilling. ("God knows," he said in November 1963, "I'm still wishing something would happen to get me out of all this. It's all a little frightening.") He confesses to uncertainty about the value of his remedies and even about the content of them. His right hand isn't always sure of what his right hand is doing—to wit, this from *Newsweek,* October 21, 1963:

Goldwater [in the course of an interview with Benjamin Bradlee, head of the magazine's Washington Bureau] solved one glaring inconsistency with a single telephone call. He was asked why he had voted for the six-billion dollar agricultural appropriations bill late last month, after he had ceaselessly called for a "prompt and final

termination of the farm-subsidy program." Goldwater denied that
he had done so. When he was shown that he had been paired for
the bill, he called the clerk of the Senate and had his vote changed
to no.

What's going on here, anyway? All the oracles are telling us
that this man is very likely to be the Republican candidate for
President in 1964. Are they serious? The answer is that indeed
they are. Is Goldwater himself serious? The question may be
irrelevant—since he is where he is, and that is that—but the
answer is not irrelevant, for whatever Goldwater is or is not has
become relevant to the rest of us. Is he, to begin with, serious
about his conservatism or is he a mere vote-hustler who, as he
once put it, likes "to go hunting where the ducks are" and figures
that there are quite a few Conservative ducks in this country? In
the light of this explanation of how he and Senator Javits could
work both sides of the street on civil rights and states' rights, the
answer would seem to be that he is a vote-hustler and not much
else. Despite all the joking about it, the word "principle" does
mean something more than protective ambiguity even to some of
the most practical of our politicians. They all dissemble now and
then, and some dissemble most of the time, but on the questions
they consider of the highest importance, most of them are guided
most of the time by an approach less foxy than the one advo-
cated by Goldwater. In his case, one would suppose that "states'
rights," which is at the core of his conservatism, would be something on which he wouldn't play footsie with Javits. There was,
to be sure, something engaging about his frankness in letting us
in on the game. There was even, in a way, something redeeming
about it. It set him apart from those who sham around the clock
and do it with an air of unrelenting piety. But the ground on
which his candor sets him lies pretty low. Senator Joe McCarthy
could be candid, too, but McCarthy was, in the deepest sense, a
rebel without a cause, and he never pretended to have a clue to
any "ancient and tested truths" on which the whole structure of
modern society should be based. George Washington Plunkitt,

the Tammany Clausewitz, explained political strategy much as
Goldwater has,* but Plunkitt never regarded himself as a statesman and wouldn't have been caught dead saying, as Goldwater
has said, "Surely the first obligation of a political thinker is to
understand the nature of man." Does Goldwater *really* look
upon himself as a "political thinker"? Does he believe that *he*
understands "the nature of man"? If these cruel questions were
put to him, he would, no doubt, grin, shift his weight about, roll
his eyes, and say, shucks, that his tone sure did seem to be lacking in humility when he wrote that.

Yet he writes and has written for him endless yards of this
high-sounding stuff, and he reads it from platforms everywhere,
and publishes it three times a week in dozens of newspapers, in
a column called "How Do You Stand, Sir?" It is decent of him,
and amusing for us, to have him now and then spill the beans
and tell us that the column is mostly written by Stephen
Shadegg, a friend who does literary carpentry and other odd
jobs for him while he, Goldwater, travels about "with a briefcase
filled with Mickey Spillane." One is somewhat disarmed—and
one wonders why *he* is not. Why, if all this is the case, does he
go on sitting in wrathful judgment on everyone from Plato to
Rousseau to John Maynard Keynes and John Dewey? The man
is dealing—I must revert to the word again, at the peril of
sounding not just grave but downright grim—with terribly
serious matters. Our relationship with the Soviet Union is a very

---

* Plunkitt was an early advocate of public ownership of utilities, which
Goldwater opposes. "I am," he explained, "for municipal ownership on
one condition: that the civil-service law be repealed. It's a grand idea—
the city ownin' the railroads, the gas works, and all that. Just see how
many thousands of new places there would be for the workers in Tammany! Why there would be almost enough to go around if no civil-
service law stood in the way." His views were set forth in press conferences and lectures delivered while he was having his shoes shined
on a bootblack stand just outside City Hall in New York. His Boswell
was William L. Riordon, a New York *Post* reporter who took it all down
and in 1905 published it in *Plunkitt of Tammany Hall,* an indispensable
work that was reissued by Alfred A. Knopf in 1948.

serious matter. On it, we have Goldwater, in an interview in the Sunday *Times* of London for July 21, 1963:

Q. Is my impression correct that you are against negotiating with the Russians?
A. I'm not against negotiating with the Russians. I'm against negotiating with the Russians who are in power today. . . . I don't think they're honest. . . . I see no advantage in meeting with them. . . . [The] average American is fed up with negotiations.

American education is another serious matter. On it, Goldwater, writing in *Human Events,* April 27, 1963: "The problem of adequate classrooms and better teacher salaries have all but disappeared." And, from the *Congressional Record* of September 3, 1963: "It is evident [that] increased school expenditures have kept pace with increased school needs."

One account of what's going on has been offered by Walter Lippmann, who thinks he observes a quite familiar process at work. Goldwater, he has written, is not a "fanatic of the extreme right but an ambitious politician [who is] reshaping himself for the political realities of this country." Lippmann thinks that Goldwater is little more than a vote-hustler and that his conservatism, whether or not he is serious about it, will not survive his acquaintance with the fact that there are not enough Conservative ducks to elect him. The great majority of enfranchised ducks are waddling about in the center, and the hunter must go after them there. Or, as Gore Vidal, using a different metaphor, put it, "When the Presidential virus attacks the system, there is a tendency for the patient in his fever to move from the Right or the Left to the Center, where the curative votes are, where John Kennedy now is." In Goldwater's backing and filling, in his unashamed switches and revisions, in his efforts at accommodation with his sworn enemies, Lippmann sees Goldwater on the move and in this finds great satisfaction, since he believes that the process insures moderation and continuity in policy. "It is interesting," he writes, "to watch him and comforting to think that the system is working so well."

If the system could be depended upon to work according to Lippmann's understanding of it, there would be little reason to pay much attention to Goldwater or to what he is saying. There would, in fact, be not much reason to take any candidate very seriously. There would be little point in discussing the Goldwater of today if we knew that by mid-1964 this Goldwater will have ceased to exist, having been transformed into a politician almost indistinguishable from Nelson Rockefeller, Richard M. Nixon, George Romney, William Scranton, and the rest. It would seem hardly worthwhile to look closely at Goldwater's conservatism if it is a garment he is about to shed. It would be idle to raise questions about his capacity for logic or about his sense of responsibility if history is going to impose upon him its own logic and the kind of responsibility it imposes on all men, in the view of Lippmann and a good many others, as they near that august office.

There is a good deal to be said in support of the Lippmann thesis. There is a force at work not only in American politics, but also in life itself that drives ambitious men toward the crowded center of things. Where the measure of success is the degree of public acceptance, men seeking success will move from the far-out, heretical, kooky, dissenting fringes toward the safe, conformist middle. And there is another side of it: the closer a man gets to the Presidency or any other station in life, the more appreciative he becomes of the limitations on initiative. Politics, Bismarck said, is the art of the possible; for the political artist, the beginning of wisdom, generally, is the knowledge that less is possible than he thought before he began to acquire any wisdom. And, to get more specific about it, it has been true, in this country in recent years, that the largest and most dangerous of our conflicts have been resolved well in advance of national elections, so that, on the first Tuesday after the first Monday of each quadrennial year, the Presidential constituency has been confronted with a choice between two men who are quite close to being in fundamental agreement with each other. The difficulty in applying the Lippmann thesis is that it has never been known to work out in a case quite like this one. The Lippmann "system" has "worked," but not quite as he describes it. The resolution of conflict has been in the choice of candidates, not in the "reshaping" of candidates by themselves. Candidates who have stood, at the outset, at a considerable distance from the center have simply been rejected in favor of candidates who already were at, or near, the center. Robert Taft modified certain of his views in his later years, and perhaps a case could be made that this was a move toward the center (though as good a case could be made that, far from being a denial of his conservatism, it was an aspect of it), but the fact, in any event, is that he was passed over four times for the nomination. Wendell Willkie, Thomas E. Dewey, and Dwight D. Eisenhower needed no basic alterations.

If the system worked in such a way as to produce a "new" Goldwater, there would be no sense in looking hard at the "old" one. If, on the other hand, it works according to Oscar Handlin's understanding of it*—that is to say, by excluding men like Goldwater—one would be led to say that, since he can't possibly get the nomination, he should be looked upon as a mere curiosity, a specimen, an interesting and politically exotic product of American life in the mid-twentieth century but scarcely as a significant or pivotal figure.

My own present feeling is that the prospect for Goldwater's elimination is better than the prospect for his taking himself in hand and making himself over to suit the New York *Times*. Despite all the evidences of frivolity in the man, there are also evidences of integrity. He has been steadfast in his adherence to

---

* Handlin describes the process in *The Americans*: "The crucial battles occurred in the nominating conventions in which the electorate were only observers. The dynamic force in those gatherings was the desire to blur rather than to define differences. Candidates—from Taft to Goldwater, from Wallace to [Richard] Russell, [W. Averell] Harriman, and [Hubert] Humphrey—who were identified with a distinctive position—were dangerous. They were certain to lose some votes. The party managers preferred a moderate nominee who would attract support from every sector of the population."

some of the most politically awkward of his views. The entire political case for Goldwater rests on his ability to carry the South, or the better part of the South. He does not advance this strategy by proposing the sale of the Tennessee Valley Authority to private interests. Yet he will not budge an inch from his position that the government should unload the TVA. The polls that encourage him to press on with his candidacy also show that the Treaty of Moscow—the agreement to prohibit nuclear and thermonuclear explosions in the atmosphere, in outer space, and in the oceans of the earth—is a very popular treaty, as treaties go. When it was before the Senate, in the fall of 1963, Goldwater hemmed and hawed for a while and finally offered a reservation to the effect that the terms of the treaty be honored only when the last Soviet troops had been withdrawn from Cuba. At the same time, he announced that he would not cast his vote to consent even if the reservation was adopted by the Senate. Whatever may be said of Goldwater's judgment or of his seriousness about serious matters, there appears to be something other than outright opportunism in the man that militates against easy "reshaping."

It ain't for life, and it may be fun.

> —Goldwater, in an undated letter to his brother, Robert, soon after deciding, in 1949, to go into politics

I have been listening to the voices of the people—people no longer asleep. . . . Their message has been heard and understood. The people are now eager for a leader who will . . . mobilize the moral force of one-hundred and eighty million.

> —Goldwater, quoted in *Mr. Conservative,* by Jack Bell, a biography published in 1962

* LIFE OF A SALESMAN, OR A ROUGH OUTLINE
FOR AN UNDEFINITIVE BIOGRAPHY

November 22, 1963

Barry Morris Goldwater was born in Phoenix, Arizona, on January 1, 1909, the first child of Baron and Josephine (nee Williams) Goldwater. Goldwaters have been prominent Arizona merchants for a little over a century. The Senator's grandfather Michael left Poland in 1847, lived for a while in Paris and London, and—accompanied by a younger brother Joseph—came to the United States in 1852, when he was thirty. After a few years of fortune-hunting in California, Michael settled in the Arizona territory. In 1862, he began work in a general merchandise store in La Paz, and by 1867 the store was his. His brother joined him, and the La Paz enterprise was known as J. Goldwater & Bro. That same year they opened a branch in Phoenix and three years later another in Prescott. Stores named Goldwaters (no apostrophe) prosper today in Phoenix, Prescott, and Scottsdale; they are no longer family concerns, however, having been sold to a chain a few years back.

The Senator's father was a small, dandified man who wore a pince-nez, used cologne with abandon, gambled aggressively, and much preferred Edwardian interiors to Arizona exteriors. He died in 1929. In 1907, he had married a trained nurse who had come to Arizona from Nebraska to recover from tuberculosis. A rangy and rugged woman, despite her early history of consumption, she still enjoys the salubrious Arizona climate and at ninety or thereabouts rejoices in her son's present eminence.

It is said that she had a far larger influence over the three Goldwater children—the Senator has a younger brother, Robert, and a younger sister, Carolyn—than her husband did. She enjoyed camping, hunting, and other activities that her husband looked upon with disdain.

Goldwater attended the public schools of Phoenix, Staunton Military Academy, in Virginia, and, for part of a year, the University of Arizona, at Tucson. He was by his own account an indifferent student. His departure from the university followed shortly upon the death of his father, and it has often been said that he withdrew from college in order to manage the family's business interests. He has himself scotched this story. In a commencement address at Staunton three years ago, he explained that he had withdrawn in his freshman year because "I could easily see [that] I'd probably be the next twenty years getting out. Therefore, I gave it up and went to work." He joined the family business, but not as an executive. The firm, according to Stephen Shadegg, author of one of many admiring biographies, *Barry Goldwater: Freedom Is His Flight Plan,* "was under the capable management of Sam Wilson, who had been with the organization since 1909." Goldwater, Shadegg writes, "went to work in the Phoenix store as a junior clerk." He could not have remained one very long. In 1937, when he was twenty-eight, he became president, a title he held until 1953, when he was elected to the United States Senate. His record as an entrepreneur appears to have been creditable, though a bit short of spectacular. His name is associated with one merchandising coup. This was in the field of men's wear—in which, it may be worth noting, another American statesman, Harry S. Truman, conspicuously failed to achieve anything but bankruptcy. In 1947 or thereabouts, Goldwater conceived and put on the market a product which he called "Antsy Pants"—underdrawers decorated with red ants rampant. The symbolism seems barren of political meaning—though in point of fact the man who apparently first spoke of "ants in the pants" was the late General Hugh L. Johnson, a salty controversialist who was himself known as Old

Ironpants and had served Franklin Roosevelt's New Deal as head of the National Recovery Administration. *The American Treasury,* edited by Clifton Fadiman, gives General Johnson the credit for the phrase and dates his first use of it in 1939.* The Goldwater Stores were sold to the Associated Dry Goods Corporation a few years ago, but the conscience of American conservatism still sits as chairman of the board. It is not known whether he sits in Antsy Pants. It may be said that in general his dress is appropriately conservative—or inappropriately liberal—at least when he is in the East, where he normally dresses in a style associated with the Ivy League colleges, of which he often says unkind things. Way out west, he affects the regional style with a vengeance—though close inspection suggests at least the possibility that it is the regional style as interpreted by Abercrombie & Fitch.

The Senator was brought up not in his father's faith, which was Jewish (Orthodox), but in his mother's, which was Christian (Protestant Episcopal). He remains a communicant of Trinity Cathedral in Phoenix, though despite the spirituality of his writings ("The laws of God and nature have no dateline") he is an infrequent churchgoer. In 1934, he married Margaret Johnson, of Muncie, Indiana, the daughter of R. P. Johnson, president of the Warner Gear Company, which was later to be merged with the Borg-Warner Corporation, with Mrs. Goldwater's father as executive vice-president. The Goldwaters have four children—Joanne, Barry Jr., Michael, and Margaret Jr. In

---

* Fadiman seems to think it is a variant of a seventeenth-century saying: "He has a breeze in his breech." H. L. Mencken has no comment except to cite "antseroo" as a word describing the general condition (*vide The American Language: Supplement One*). Lester V. Berrey and Melvin Van Den Bark, in *The American Thesaurus of Slang,* cite "ants in the pants" as expressive of "annoyance, vexation," "vexatious person," and "energetic or enterprising person." So much for scholarship. The link to General Johnson, though, is interesting. It should not be overlooked that General Johnson, in his days with NRA, saw to it that the Blue Eagle, the emblem of his administration, was on underwear, both male and female.

the Senator's early life, few traces are to be found of the stern rightist ideology to which he now adheres and which he promotes with such vigor. In his adolescence and youth, he was devoted to the more strenuous pursuits. At Staunton, he was captain of the swimming team, a high-scoring basketball player, and—despite his poor academic showing—a fine cadet. In 1928, indeed, he won the school's Kable Medal as the "best all-around cadet." At Arizona, he played football and was a promising freshman center. He was a gregarious youth and given at times to carousal. He was pledged to Sigma Chi and, though his experience of it was brief, he has always been a defender of the fraternity system. ("Where fraternities are not allowed, Communism flourishes," he said to the National Interfraternity Conference in Los Angeles on November 25, 1960.) A pillar of respectability in Phoenix, he has a police record in Mexico, where he once hit a Nogales officer of the law with a jar of mustard. With the onset of maturity, he turned increasingly to hobbies—photography, aviation, golf, Indian lore, sports cars, short-wave radio, and electronic improvisation, *i.e.,* a device for running the Stars and Stripes up, at sunrise, and down, at sunset, the flagpole outside his Phoenix residence, a red sandstone structure designed in the shape of an arrow and named Nun-i-Kin, or, translated from the Navajo, Home on the Hill. The Navajos are a minority he cultivates. He has mastered some of the language and many of the tribal dances, and on his left hand bears four Navajo tattoos. His Navajo name is Barry Sundust.

To say that there were in Goldwater's early life few portents of what may now be called Goldwaterism is not to say that he held some other view on questions of public policy. It is merely to say that there were few signs of political concern and none whatever of zeal. Yet in retrospect it may be held that the tree grew pretty much as the twig was bent. Though the family tradition was Democratic (Goldwater's uncle Morris was a founder of the party in Arizona), the outlook, as befitted the family's mercantile interests and accumulating wealth, was conservative. As a young businessman, Goldwater found the New Deal displeasing, and he once addressed himself to its leader in a deeply aggrieved tone. On June 23, 1938, he contributed a "guest editorial" to the Phoenix *Gazette*. It bore the title "A Fireside Chat with Mr. Roosevelt" and the signature of the father of Antsy Pants, who was, he said, "very interested in the queer antics in Washington." He went on:

Are you going further down into that morass that you have led us into, or are you going back to the good old American way of doing things where business is trusted, where labor earns more, where we take care of our unemployed, and where a man is elected to public office because he is a good man for the job and not because he commands your good will and a few dollars of taxpayers' money? I like the old-fashioned way of being an American a lot better than the way we are headed now.

A fair enough sample of entrepreneurial, or American Liberty League, rhetoric, *circa* 1938, but superficial inquiry discloses no record of political engagement, of lust for power, or of any really passionate protest. The one commitment he seems always to have honored is to the military life and the military view of things, which he had first absorbed at Staunton. He had held a reserve commission as a second lieutenant of infantry since 1930 but, as an enthusiastic flyer, he wished to join the Army Air Corps, and he did. He was ineligible for combat, but he made a splendid record ferrying bombers to India on a route that included stops in the Azores, Casablanca, and Karachi. He was mustered out as a lieutenant colonel, but almost immediately upon his discharge—and return to merchandising—he organized and became chief of staff of the Arizona Air National Guard. Major General Goldwater (USAF Reserve) is at present the commanding officer of the 9999th Combined Air Force Reserve Squadron, a unit made up of Members of Congress and congressional employees. He has never sought to conceal his partiality for the military as against the civilian point of view. In defending his vote against the 1963 Treaty of Moscow, he said, "I have lived too long with reality, too long with the men who are dedicated to our defense [to] discard all that I am and all that I know."

Goldwater first put a toe in political waters in 1949, when he ran on a nonpartisan reform ticket for the City Council in Phoenix. He has attributed his decision to become involved partly to a growing sense of civic virtue, partly to the mounting tedium of an ex-Air Corps colonel running a dry-goods business that ran itself in postwar Phoenix. The ticket he ran on was committed to firm action against brothel keepers, bookmakers, and other undesirables. He served two terms, and his record as a city father has of late been the subject of some controversy. Perhaps to offset the present criticism of him as an ally of Southern racists, his supporters have maintained that he did much to better the lot of Negroes in Phoenix. It is said, for example, that he played a large role in desegregating the public schools of that city. Contemporary records do not bear out this contention. No one has been able to find a Goldwater statement on the subject in the City Council minutes or elsewhere. In October 1951, he contributed four hundred dollars to the National Association for the Advancement of Colored People, which was at the time pressing a lawsuit to desegregate the schools, but civil-rights leaders fail to recall any political help or encouragement he gave them. His membership in the NAACP lapsed in 1955. He has himself frequently said that he was responsible for "desegregating" the municipal airport. It is a fact that the City Council during Goldwater's time ordered an airport restaurant, the Sky Chef, to cease refusing service to Negroes. In the council minutes and in newspaper accounts, there is no mention of Goldwater taking any stand. (On September 23, 1952, he touched on the subject in a single sentence, an inquiry. "Mr. Mayor," he said, "because of occasional absences from the city, I would like to ask the attorney what is the status of the Sky Chef segregation situation?")

Certain aspects of his record appear to be beyond dispute. It is said that he rose above self-interest in opposing municipal parking lots in downtown Phoenix. Most Phoenix merchants favored this particular welfare program. Goldwater stoutly opposed it. He felt that it smacked of socialism. He also led the resistance to a parents' lobby that wished to withhold a license for the unrestricted sale of beer in a supermarket two hundred feet from the West Phoenix High School. Goldwater held firm against their pressure, arguing that parents should raise children impervious to temptation. Moreover, he pointed out, "those who are going to drink will find ways of doing it one way or another." His was the victorious cause, by one vote.

In 1950, Goldwater entered partisan politics as the campaign manager for Howard Pyle, a popular radio announcer who that year won election as governor of Arizona. This was not quite what Goldwater had planned when he and Pyle joined forces several months earlier. Goldwater wanted very much to be governor, and early in 1950 sought Pyle's counsel. Pyle was an Arizona celebrity with wide and varied acquaintances throughout the state. He was much admired for having conceived and splendidly executed the Grand Canyon Easter Sunrise broadcasts—a celebration of the resurrection carried nationwide by the National Broadcasting Company. He also had a program in which he read poetry of a most affecting character. His political experience was modest, even alongside Goldwater's—in fact, he had none—but he had traveled about the state a great deal entertaining Rotarians, Kiwanians, Lions, Elks, Odd Fellows, and such, and he was able to report to Goldwater, a close friend, that things were looking up for Republicans in Arizona. Goldwater agreed, and said he would run for governor if Pyle would manage his campaign. Pyle said he would lend himself to Goldwater's ambition if, in return, Goldwater would support him in a campaign for the Senate two years later. This was the plan, until Pyle appeared before a convention of Arizona Young Republicans. He evidently surpassed himself in honeyed eloquence, and the Young Republicans surrendered themselves then and there and named him as their candidate. Their elders were impressed by the response the poetry reader had drawn, and thus it was Pyle, not Goldwater, who won the nomination for the governorship in 1950.

Goldwater was, as always, sporting. He had wanted the governorship badly, according to friends, and was interested in no other office. He agreed to manage Pyle's campaign against the Democratic candidate, Mrs. Ana Frohmiller, and he provided not only support and counsel, but transportation. He and Pyle covered the state in a red-white-and-blue Bonanza 767-Bravo, with Goldwater at the controls. Pyle won by three thousand votes (50.8 per cent) and served as governor until 1954, when he was defeated by former Senator Ernest McFarland, who two years earlier had lost his Senate seat to Goldwater. Pyle, who was later to turn up in Washington as an adviser to President Eisenhower, had some sort of falling-out with Goldwater. "As long as Howard Pyle was governor," Goldwater has said, "he never once sought my advice or asked me for a suggestion in connection with the political affairs of the Governor's office." Goldwater nevertheless had put Arizona Republicans in his debt and had no trouble getting the nomination for Senator in 1952. He rode in on Eisenhower's coattails. Eisenhower carried Arizona by forty-two thousand votes, Goldwater by seven thousand—or 51.4 per cent.

In his first campaign and in his early years, Goldwater was by no means the militant he is today. He had yet, it would seem, to come upon the verities he now proclaims. It was not that he was notably less "conservative" than he is now. He was conservative enough to have received contributions from H. L. Hunt, of Dallas, and a Chicago extremist group named Americans for America.* But he did not, then, present himself as a

---

* He also received a five-hundred-dollar contribution from a Phoenix friend known to Goldwater as William Nelson. In gratitude, Goldwater inscribed a photograph to Nelson, who a few days later visited Goldwater with the photograph, which he tore to pieces in Goldwater's presence. According to Goldwater, he then revealed himself as the notorious Willie Bioff, a former Hollywood labor racketeer, who had done time for ex-

qualified exponent of "the laws of God and nature" or as the scourge of "the worldwide Communist menace." He had backed Eisenhower against Robert Taft for the 1952 Republican nomination, and he now and then sounded, as so many other Republicans of the period did, as if he wanted to save the New Deal by putting it under sound business management. In his first speech as a candidate, he addressed himself "to all sincere men and women who are concerned with retaining the social gains which have been made in the past twenty years." He went on about the "gains":

We reestablished our new system of social security [!] and unemployment insurance and old-age assistance, aid to dependent children and to the blind. We established the F.H.A. to make long term [home] financing available. . . . We found a method of regulating the trading of securities. These things have been of great benefit to the people. [No] responsible Republican, and certainly not this Republican has any . . . desire to abolish any of them.

Six years later, addressing a Dallas audience, he was to say:

The inescapable and harmful by-product of such operations as relief, social security, collective bargaining, and public housing has been the weakening of the individual personality and of self-reliance.

That was after three years in the Senate. The conservative and his conscience must have met sometime between 1952 and 1956. In his first year in the Senate, he was not a reliable member of the conservative coalition. On one key matter he opposed it; he voted to outlaw the Senate filibuster. Nor was he as contemptuous of accommodation in the Cold War as he is today. While Richard Nixon and John Foster Dulles were trying to prepare American opinion for armed intervention on the French side in the Indochina war, Goldwater was proposing an amendment to the foreign-aid bill that would cut France off without

---

tortion and pandering. Westbrook Pegler has written that it was Bioff who educated Goldwater in the "coercive, terroristic, and often criminal methods of union bosses." Bioff died in 1955 from the blast of a bomb placed in his pickup truck.

a dime unless she gave "satisfactory assurances" that she would "free" Vietnam, Laos, and Cambodia. This seemed in line with his attitude, in his first campaign, toward the war in Korea. At that time, he insisted that his opponent, Ernest McFarland, "accept his share of the responsibility for the more than 117,000 American boys who have been killed, wounded, or captured in Korea." He challenged his opponent "to find anywhere within the boundaries of Arizona or within the borders of the United States a single mother or father who counts these casualties as cheap—who'd be willing to exchange the life of one American boy for the nine Communists or the 900 Communists or 9,000,-000 Communists."

The late Robert Taft and Lyndon Johnson are the only two Senators of recent times who have had distinguished careers as legislators and have come close to the Presidency. Richard Nixon, of course, served only a third of a term. John F. Kennedy served a term and a third, and his record fell far short of being commensurate with his gifts. Goldwater is now rounding out his second full term, and in these twelve years he seems scarcely to have attempted to achieve distinction of any kind within the Senate, unless it may be said that being the most consistent naysayer in many decades is distinction of a sort. There were not many votes like the one on the filibuster. As a rule, he missed no opportunity to oppose legislation embodying any sort of government commitment to anything but military power. He was almost as much in opposition to the Republican administration as he was to the Democratic administration. In April 1957, he broke sharply with President Eisenhower, saying that the President's requests for appropriations were "abominably high" and, speaking of his party's financial stewardship, that "it constitutes a betrayal of the people's trust." Later, when asked to comment on the President's brother Milton as a possible party leader, he said, "One Eisenhower in a generation is enough."

His everlasting naysaying on the Senate floor was accompanied by very low expenditures of Senatorial energy off the floor. To some extent, inactivity was a requirement of his political philosophy. A man who believes that the government should go out of business is not likely to find himself much concerned about helping it to solve its problems. Studies made by the *Congressional Quarterly* show Goldwater in both the Eisenhower and the Kennedy administrations with a one-hundred-per-cent record of voting against legislation enlarging the federal government's participation. His support of the Eisenhower administration dropped steadily in its closing years. In the Eighty-sixth Congress, the last one in the Eisenhower years, he was on the President's side only 52 per cent of the time. He has often said that his proudest moment as a Senator came when he voted with the opposition—consisting of himself alone—against the Kennedy-Ervin labor-reform bill in 1959. Thirty Republicans and sixty Democrats agreed on the measure. In *The Conscience of a Conservative,* he describes this vote as "the most important of my Senate career." *

At the Republican convention in 1960, Goldwater got, on the final roll call, ten votes, as against Richard Nixon's 1,321. If fervor had been redeemable in votes, he would have done considerably better, but that can be said of many losers, and the Goldwater-for-President movement, which had been organized mainly as a display of ultraright strength, seemed to have little behind it. Goldwater was gallant in defeat, and campaigned vigorously for Nixon, which disappointed some of his supporters. Goldwater, said Kent Cortney, the editor of the *Independent American* and a member of the John Birch Society, "has been tainted with socialism." Nevertheless, "Goldwater in '64" bumper stickers began turning up all over the place within a few weeks after Nixon's defeat, and there began, in early 1961, what many

* This, as it happens, was not an anti-Eisenhower vote. On the contrary, when the Senator explained his position to the President, he was told by Eisenhower that "If I had been with you as a member of the Senate, I would have voted as you did." In one of his rare appeals to the public, Eisenhower made a televised speech calling for another bill. The House never voted on the Kennedy-Ervin bill. Instead, it produced one of its own—the Landrum-Griffin bill, which passed House and Senate. Goldwater was one of ninety-five Senators voting aye.

authorities regarded as an extraordinary and menacing resurgence of ultraconservatism, with Goldwater as the rallying point. Whether it was a genuine resurgence is open to question. The rightists were little heard from during Eisenhower's tenure because no Republican officeholders wished to be associated with a movement that was as contemptuous of the Republican President as it was of any of his Democratic critics. With Eisenhower out, Republicans who leaned toward the far right could be less restricted in their choice of words and of friends; with Kennedy in, they once more had a plausible villain. Whether the extremists were growing in numbers or merely making more noise (which at times is symptomatic of a decline in numbers), their leaders found a basis of agreement in the "Goldwater in '64" crusade.

How large a part Goldwater played in helping them toward this unity is far from clear. He had for some years been consorting with the extremists and defending them whenever they were under attack, which was almost all the time. There is little evidence, though, that Presidential ambition was the spur. In politics, it is common to assume that ambition explains anything that is not easily explained in some other way, but there is no real evidence that Goldwater's ambition is at all unusual. On the contrary, it seems clear that its intensity does not approach that of John F. Kennedy at a similar stage, or that of Nelson Rockefeller today, and right now it is possible to wonder whether Goldwater really wants either the Republican nomination or the Presidency. "I have no desire for it," he told the National Press Club last year. "I don't want the job," he told a California audience this year. And although he has since said how nice it might be to run for both the Presidency and the Senate, reporters who travel around the country with him persist in believing that there is a part of him—a very large part—that resists the whole idea. At this stage, of course, what he may or may not want has little to do with what will or will not happen next year. He is the commander of an embattled army, and he must abandon command headquarters feet first or not at all. If he were to walk out, the one defense he could make would be that he did not seek command but had it thrust upon him. It would be unacceptable to the troops but not groundless. Circumstances that were entirely beyond his control account for his present position of being by far the strongest contender for the Republican nomination. There was, to begin with, the defeat of Richard M. Nixon in his attempt to win the governorship of California in 1962. This, and the bad grace with which he took defeat, seemed to eliminate Nixon, but Goldwater was not at the time the immediate gainer from Nixon's loss. Rockefeller took a commanding lead. In April 1963, the Gallup Poll reported that 43 per cent of rank-and-file Republicans favored Rockefeller for the nomination and that 26 per cent favored Goldwater. George Romney, the Mormon automotive wizard who became governor of Michigan in 1962, was favored by 13 per cent. A month later, Dr. Gallup announced that Goldwater had overcome Rockefeller's lead; he drew 35 per cent to Rockefeller's 30, with Romney pulling up to 22.* The newspapers played this switch of positions as if it were an ideological revolution—the Republican Party, it was argued, had switched from the candidate who stood farthest to the left to the one who stood farthest right. There is no reason to question the essential accuracy of the polls, but it is perfectly clear that what had moved Goldwater into the lead was neither his own political activity, which had been no more intensive than at any other time in the past couple of years, nor a sudden shift in Republican thinking. The only development of any note within the Republican Party in the period between the two soundings was the marriage of the recently divorced Governor of New York to the

* It is interesting to note that Romney gained almost as much as Goldwater—8 per cent as against 9. Goldwater moved into first place in May, but he was 13 per cent below Rockefeller in April. Goldwater's lead over Rockefeller in May was nothing like Rockefeller's lead over Goldwater in April—as a glance at the above figures will show.

recently divorced Mrs. Margaretta Murphy. Goldwater was the beneficiary of a highly unideological development.*

There were, to be sure, developments that could, in a way, be regarded as ideological. Goldwater's appeal to his party's Warwicks is enhanced by their knowledge that he could have a better chance than any other Republican of winning electoral votes in the South. But this was hardly a serious consideration before the civil-rights crisis in the spring that also witnessed the change in Nelson Rockefeller's domestic arrangements. Goldwater bore as little responsibility for the first development as for the second. The one large and deliberate contribution he has made to his own advancement is a speaking schedule so heavy

* The applicable principle here is *post hoc, ergo propter hoc.* There seems not to be room for the slightest doubt that Rockefeller's decline was a consequence of Rockefeller's marriage to Mrs. Murphy. There is, however, plenty of room for doubt as to the role of mores and morality in the thinking of those who switched, in a manner of speaking, from Lenin to the Czar. Was it really that a large number of people were scandalized? Or was it that a large number felt that a still larger number *would be* scandalized? My view—quite unsubstantiated by polls or research of any sort—is that Rockefeller's remarriage became an issue not because of the remarriage but because of Rockefeller. Among those Republicans who favored him in April were many who had no particular use for him but were carried along by the knowledge that he was the Governor of New York, that he was personally attractive, that he was rich beyond dreams of avarice, that fortune had smiled upon him in ways too numerous for counting. They were not happy with his chatter about civil rights and economic growth, and the rest of it, but they thought they saw a winner in him, and they could not resist a winner. They had, in short, no reason for not being for him. But in the spring he—and the former Mrs. Murphy—gave them a reason, a chance to cop a plea. They were bandwagon travelers eager for any excuse to transfer. Rockefeller gave them what they wanted. In a country in which every third or fourth marriage ends in divorce, it is not easy to believe that divorce is a politically disqualifying factor. But divorce doesn't help much, and in the prevailing uncertainty over what the American people feel or don't feel about the private lives of public men, it was natural that a number of politicians who never liked Rockefeller anyway should advise the poll takers that Rockefeller had doomed himself. Their saying so helped to make it so.

that any man who would take it on must automatically come under suspicion of harboring the very largest of ambitions. Even here, though, Goldwater's case is a rather special one. In 1955, he was elected chairman of the Republican Senatorial Campaign Committee—a position that requires its occupant to go any-place from sea to shining sea where a hat may be passed for contributions to Republican senatorial campaigns. Goldwater held this demanding office until this year, and worked at it with astonishing vigor and with what to him must have been gratifying results. (In those eight years, during which the Presidency was lost and large numbers of Republican governors, congressmen, and state legislators were replaced by Democrats, there was a net loss of only two Republican seats in the Senate.) Whether or not Goldwater is an uncommonly ambitious politician, he is unquestionably an energetic one. Long before anyone felt compelled to take him seriously as a candidate in 1964, he had logged a million miles and made thousands of speeches —the calculations are his—and for this reason was almost certainly justified in saying, as he did last month, "I don't think anyone in this Party knows more Republicans than I do." He has also said, "This accumulation of Republican friends wasn't done with the idea of using it for anything except getting Republicans elected. . . . It came as a by-product of my just doing my job as a Republican." His celebrity in the party's ranks—as distinct from his present standing among candidates for the party's nomination—was won at a time when his main quarry was cash and when he might almost as reasonably have aspired to be King of Spain as President of the United States.

It does not seem very difficult to explain Goldwater's progress from the mid-fifties to the mid-sixties. When he entered the Senate, in 1953, the only Republican leaders of note were President Eisenhower and Senator Taft. The President was the President because his constituency was bipartisan. Senator Taft was a defeated man and a dying one. In the eight Eisenhower years, only Nixon and Rockefeller attracted followings of any size. Goldwater acquired, as he said, a lot of Republican friends, but the friends had prior commitments. Nixon suffered two major defeats. Rockefeller made a gross miscalculation of some sort and dropped 13 per cent in the Gallup ratings. Goldwater, who a few months previously had been running a poor third, moved to the top by a double default and has held it nicely for six months. He is attractive, he is agreeable, he is available. He is articulate in conversation but an indifferent speaker and a fumbling debater. Even when his words are listless, though, and his line of argument cloudy, his manner is unfailingly ingratiating.

Goldwater's victories thus far have not been in doctrinal combat, but it is doctrine that has made a combatant out of him. He represents a small state, and, unless his friends in the party are to be regarded as a power unit in themselves, he controls no important piece of political machinery. He has few favors to grant and few to withhold. Unlike Governor Rockefeller, unlike the Vice-President in 1960, he cannot conscript political laborers. He commands only volunteers. Those who now toil in the vineyard for Goldwater do so because they like the message he brings; if he should bring a very different one, they would be perfectly free to remove the Goldwater stickers from their car bumpers and occupy themselves in some other way. In numbers, the volunteers may not constitute a very impressive force, but they are an indispensable one, and to them doctrine is just about everything. They have allies in Goldwater followers of a commoner kind—the party workers who appraise doctrines by the number of votes they are likely to win or lose. Indifferent to doctrine, they skip from Nixon, in the middle, to Rockefeller, on the left, to Goldwater, on the right, because they are looking for a winner. Those who support Goldwater now do so because they accept the view of his strategists that the only way the Republicans can win in 1964 is by carrying all the South and all the West—except, perhaps, for California. Doctrine has become crucial to this group because it is doctrine that makes Goldwater acceptable in the South and West.

A Solid South and an almost Solid West cannot prevail against a Solid East, a Solid Midwest, and California. The

Goldwater people acknowledge this, but argue that the party organizations in some of the more populous states ought to be able to deliver for the party candidate, whoever he is. This is the proposition, one can be sure, that will be most hotly disputed in the next several months, and Goldwater's doctrine will be at the center of the controversy.

A man's politics are, primarily, the product of his mind.

—Goldwater, *The Conscience of a Conservative*

So far as any man is competent to contend against our sea of troubles, Mr. Goldwater is endowed with the sort of brain that is required for our modern Presidency.

—Russell Kirk, "The Mind of Barry Goldwater," an essay in *Confessions of a Bohemian Tory*

* THE MINDS OF BARRY G., OR THE HAZARDS OF CATERED RHETORIC

July 3, 1964

Wherever he has gone this year, Barry Goldwater has been held to account for the strident language and impolitic opinions of a man named Barry Goldwater. The first Goldwater, the flesh-and-blood candidate, insists that the second is a fiction—a fright created by Nelson Rockefeller, William Scranton, the New York *Herald Tribune,* and other pillars of the "Eastern establishment." The Goldwater they keep talking about is a man who favors the use of nuclear weapons in brush-fire wars ("I'd drop a low-yield nuclear bomb on Chinese supply lines in North Vietnam"),* the dismantling of the Social Security system ("I do not propose to promote welfare. . . . Let welfare be a private concern"),† United States withdrawal from the United Nations ("Interviewer: Would you, as President, favor getting out of the United Nations? Goldwater: I would"),‡ and the sale at auction of the Tennessee Valley Authority ("I think TVA should be turned over to free enterprise, even if they could only get one dollar for it").** The Senator says that he cannot be talking about him; these, he says, are not his aims. When opponents and critics have cited what they claimed to be the record, he has replied that they are citing a nonrecord or a falsified one.

* *Newsweek,* May 20, 1963.
† *The Conscience of a Conservative.*
‡ WOR-TV, New York, May 20, 1963.
** *Congressional Record,* 1961, p. 12987.

Asked on February 12 if he had *ever* favored withdrawal from the United Nations, he said, "This is as complete a falsehood as I have ever heard." In his latest book, *Where I Stand,* he says, "I believe the United States should make the fullest possible use of its membership in the U.N." And "I favor a sound Social Security System, and I want to see it strengthened." And "The Tennessee Valley Authority is an enterprise unique in our nation. Some of its elements have been successful and should be continued."

Either someone is lying or there are two Goldwaters. I believe that the second explanation explains more. There *are* two Goldwaters—at least that many. There is, on the one hand, the Senator on the hustings, the agreeable man with the easy, breezy Aw Shucks Western manner who speaks in rightist platitudes but has only a loose grip on ideology and not, apparently, much interest in it. And there is, on the other hand, the dour authoritarian polemicist whose name is signed to *The Conscience of a Conservative, Why Not Victory?,* and many hundreds of articles, columns, and press releases so heavily freighted with smarmy theology and invocations of Natural Law ("Right-to-work laws derive from Natural Law") that they have won for the Senator the warm approval of Archduke Otto of Austria, and the admiration of the ranking ideologues of the Franco regime in Spain. There is the Goldwater who can dispose of a large national problem by saying "If we get back to readin', writin', and 'rithmetic and an occasional little whack where it will help, then I think our educational system will take care of itself." And there is the portentous Goldwater, abounding in theory: "We have forgotten that the proper function of the school is to transmit the cultural heritage of one generation to another. . . . The fundamental explanation of this distortion of values is that we have forgotten that purpose of education. [It] is not to educate, or elevate, *society,* but rather to educate the *individual.* . . . [We must] recapture the lost arts of learning."

One Goldwater sounds like a George Babbitt from the Grand Canyon country: "Just what does it mean to be 'modern,' anyway? I think of myself as modern in the true meaning, as out-lined in the dictionaries. My brother and I have just built a new store. I am building a new home. I fly an airplane. I like new things and new gadgets." The other sounds like a miterless Bishop Fulton J. Sheen: "Conservatism, we are told, is out of date. The charge is preposterous, and we ought boldly to say so. The laws of God and of nature have no dateline." One may be a product of nature and the other of art, but the second has as much materiality as the first and perhaps more. But this does not mean that the first is wholly disingenuous when he claims that the other is a fiction. As a matter of fact, the second is a fiction—though the authors are Goldwater's friends, not his rivals or his enemies. The first may be a fiction too—but this suggestion opens up possibilities beyond the scope of this study.

In a sense, of course, every politician successful enough to hire a press agent and a ghost writer is two men—the one who lives inside his skin and the one who lives in newsprint. There is the corporeal Dwight Eisenhower, the old soldier who plays bridge and golf, broils steaks outdoors, and has the devil's own time making up his mind about anything. And there is—or for many years there was—James Hagerty's Eisenhower, the states-man in whose wisdom, purpose, and firm command the people could have confidence even when doctors were protecting the old soldier from any knowledge of what was going on in the world outside his hospital room. But the two Eisenhowers never provided the contrast the two Goldwaters do. They were never antagonists, never strangers to one another. Hagerty's was merely the largest and best of all possible Eisenhowers, and it was this imposing figure who won elections.

What is strange and perhaps unprecedented in the case of the two Goldwaters is that the less "real" one, the product of so much cosmetic enterprise, is the one who has turned out to be more unattractive—has turned out, actually, to be a menace to the candidate. We tend to assume that the product of the press agents and the ghostwriters will somehow appear to be more appealing, freer of blemishes, worthier of trust than the original. Otherwise, why bother? Why tamper with nature except to improve on it? But those who have brought the other Goldwater into being by putting words in his mouth have produced not a better Goldwater but, politically, a far worse one. They produced the loser of the Oregon and New Hampshire primaries and the man who continues to do so poorly in the opinion polls.

In his 1964 attempts to disown the second Goldwater, or at least shed bits and pieces of him, the candidate is being less than candid. He knows, after all, that he is the author of record of his two books and of a great deal else that his opponents have been studying more carefully than he ever seems to have done. He has shot from the hip so often and sworn in so many deputies to shoot from *their* hips that he can't possibly keep track of it all. "Oh, hell, I have ghosts all over the place," he told Stewart Alsop. He has put out as his own just about anything that has borne or seemed to bear a "conservative" tag. Once last year, he put in the *Congressional Record* the text of a speech headed "Is Conservatism Dynamic?" which he said he had delivered in Montclair, New Jersey. Actually, the speech was delivered by a scholar from Princeton, and it was largely an attack on Goldwaterism. Twelve days later, Goldwater's office said there had been a "clerical error." Goldwater had delivered no speech in Montclair.

Things got so bad late in 1963 that the staff had to take on some microfilm and punch-card people to sort out what Goldwater had been saying, or had been having said for him, over the years and to determine exactly what commitments had been made for him and by him. No progress report has been issued. Distinguishing between what he has said and what others have said for him is a problem in philosophy and morals; it is unlikely that machinery could deal with it. In his introduction to *Why Not Victory?*, he lists sixteen persons—"helpers, ghosts, call them what you will"—who were, he said, "but a few of those who provided me with the crutches I so badly need." One may wonder how on earth sixteen people (or seventeen, if Goldwater had anything to do with it) could be "but a few of those" involved in turning out a hundred-and-twenty-eight-page wafer of a book, but we scarcely need the Senator to tell us that he doesn't walk unaided. Almost everything that has ever appeared under his name has been cast in a rhetoric alien to his mode of thinking and speaking. *Why Not Victory?* and most of the columns and articles are written in a throat-grabbing pamphletese that reaches notes of shrillness far beyond Goldwater's range. These high notes have generally been supplied by "my close friend Stephen Shadegg," an ex-pulp-writer and businessman. *The Conscience of a Conservative* is written in a heavy-duty prose developed in the academy and the seminary as a vehicle for doctrinal assertion, promulgation, and dispute. To close students of that book, in which no acknowledgment of assistance was made, it was hardly a surprise to be told by Goldwater, in the introduction to its sequel, that "the guiding hand" had been that of L. Brent Bozell, a star performer for the *National Review,* a journal whose every page is filled with this combative, abrasive language.*

* Bozell's recent intellectual history has been interesting. In 1960, when he worked on *The Conscience of a Conservative,* his views seemed indistinguishable from those of others in the rightist school with which he was associated, the school led by his brother-in-law, William F. Buckley, Jr., and spoken for by the *National Review.* These people are fond of calling themselves "libertarian" conservatives, and they insist that their goal is individual liberty, or freedom. As it is put in *The Conscience of a Conservative,* "the Conservative's first concern will always be: *Are we maximizing freedom?*" Two years after this book appeared, Bozell kicked up quite a storm in rightist circles by abandoning this position. In a *National Review* article entitled "Freedom or Virtue?" he said that reflection had led him to conclude that "freedom" would not do as a conservative goal and that, indeed, freedom might have to be limited and restrained in order to provide more opportunities for "virtue," which is the ultimate value in life. Virtue is virtue, he said, whether it is personified by a man free to err or whether, as behavior, it is "a) reflexive, b) instinctive, c) coerced by state power." In this light, he reasoned, Franco's Spain (in which he had lately been living) might produce a greater sum total of virtue than a society striving, as Goldwater said he would have ours do, to "maximize freedom." "For," Bozell went on, "as the mystics tell

"There is no feeling of weakness in admitting this need for help," Goldwater, or somebody, writes in the introduction to *Why Not Victory?* "The fight for Conservatism requires the thoughts and efforts of many." This is a wild *non sequitur,* but no matter—no one really expects politicians to find all their own words, even for what is advanced as a testament of "conscience." In any case, there is a more interesting and more important question than how much or how little of Goldwater is to be found in these books. It is: How much or how little of these books is to be found in Goldwater? Must he, that is to say, stand on the ground that Bozell and others have prepared for him? We know, of course, that on some specific issues he has already left it, and we can be sure that on others he would like to. Yet he remains, and is proud to remain, a factionalist. In his votes on the test-ban treaty, the civil-rights bill, and the antipoverty bill, he held his position outside the consensus. What identified him four years ago was his extreme antifederalism in domestic affairs, and in foreign affairs his total opposition to any accommodation with the Communist states. These positions continue to give him his identity, and the question now is whether this must always be the case. Can he really be a candidate of the whole Republican Party? Could he ever be a President of all the people?

It seems likely that Goldwater himself would be at a loss for an answer to these questions. There is no evidence that he has ever considered them important or has ever given them much thought. And there is some rather impressive evidence that he has yet to make a really thorough exploration of the ground on which he stands, or has stood. One assumes, naturally, that he has at one time or another read most of what has been written for him. Much of it, in fact, he has read aloud—drawing on the

---

us, true sanctity is achieved only when man loses his freedom—when he is freed of the temptation to displease God." Bozell, according to Goldwater, worked on *Why Not Victory?,* which was also published in 1962. Early this year he sought, as a Goldwater man, a Republican nomination for congressman in Maryland. He failed to get it.

"WE SHALL OVERCOME!"

books for speech texts and depositing old speech texts in books. But "reading"—with or without lips moving—is an activity that can be carried on with varying degrees of intensity, absorption, and comprehension. Goldwater has been rather a casual student of his own works. For example, this from an interview he granted *Newsweek* last October:

> Q. In your first political book, you said that the "alliance system . . . ultimately dooms [us] to failure." But in 1962, you said that alliances can "form a great dam against the running tide. . . ." How about today?
>
> A. I would be hard put to remember what caused me to write that alliances doom us to failure.*

But the most intriguing acknowledgment of surprise and what appears to be shock comes at the end of *Why Not Victory?*, in a two-page passage headed "A Final Word." Several platoons of ghosts may have been recruited to produce this slender but bellicose tract, but one has the feeling that this epilogue is entirely the work of a Phoenix merchant who at once commands and is at the mercy of an army of zealots. "Reading over what I have written," the passage begins, "it strikes me that my tone may be lacking in humility." This is exactly on the mark. For lack of humility, no recent book with the possible exception of Norman Mailer's *Advertisements for Myself* deserves comparison with this one.

The passage continues:

> I don't know all the answers, and I have very little patience with those who pretend they do. [This at the close of a book which is

* He would have suffered no embarrassment if he had recalled what the book actually said. The *Newsweek* quotation was faulty. The argument in *The Conscience of a Conservative* was that the destruction of communism should be the aim of American policy and that the alliance system could not realize this aim because its approach was defensive. What the text says is that "This fact ultimately dooms it to failure." The interviewer replaced the "it" with "us." Goldwater could have claimed perfect consistency.

all answers and, except in its title, no questions.] None of us here in Washington knows all or even half the answers.

Your representatives in the nation's capital are not unlike you—with your doubts and faults and frailties. What was it my prep-school coach used to say in the locker room before the game to quiet our fears about the monsters we were about to meet on the gridiron? "Those guys are human—they put on their pants one leg at a time just like you."

Your Congressman, your Senators, your Cabinet members, and your President are human. I dare say—though I could not prove it to be a fact—they put on their pants one leg at a time.

Being human, they need help. Your help. After all, you elect them. You must be responsible to them. If you don't know anything about the communist conspiracy, if you think Karl Marx is Groucho's brother, if what Khrushchev is doing to the world escapes your attention because you turn right to the sports pages (I turn right to the sports pages but then I reluctantly thumb to the front of the paper), then you are not being responsible to the people you elect.

We, the elected, half lead and we half follow. . . . You are 180,000,000 voices, and I'm just one little Senator.

This is an extraordinary passage—extraordinary in its desperation, in its vulgarity, in its mindlessness, in its bottomless irresponsibility. It seems clearly the product of a direct confrontation—probably the first, perhaps the last—of the two Goldwaters. It is hard to imagine the man who wrote it (I cannot entertain the possibility that this came from anyone but the Senator himself)* even wanting to be President of the United States, but nothing is clearer than that the author of these words, at the time they were written, would have liked nothing better than to dive into the "mainstream," to accept every article of the "consensus." He is "just one little Senator" who doesn't know

* There are more things in heaven and earth than are dreamt of in my philosophy. I am now (January 1965) authoritatively advised that this affecting passage was written by someone other than Goldwater. The ghost has identified himself, and a most reputable shade he is. All I can say, in my shame, is that, if the price is right, I could use so convincing a ghost.

"even half the answers." He invites us to discount him at better than 50 per cent.

No doubt the "one little Senator" Goldwater has been silenced forever. *Pro bono publico,* one hopes so. But the 1964 candidate will urge us to make, or to allow him to make, some discounts. He can be relied upon to argue that he, like so many other leaders before him, will have to respond to the needs and events of the times and not to the imperatives found in some scraps of catered rhetoric. This is certainly a mainstream position. We do not want or expect our public men to honor campaign oratory at the expense of common sense, safety, or subsequently revealed truth. But the difficulty with Goldwater, and *for* Goldwater, is that he is not in the contemporary sense a "public man." The true Goldwater, the inner Goldwater, if there really is one, may be as flexible as a rubber band, but the Goldwater that we and he must contend with in 1964 is something else again. When this man bends, he breaks. He has said, or allowed others to say for him, things that no politician in his senses would dream of saying. Consider this incredible sentence from *Why Not Victory?*: "We should, I believe, announce in no uncertain terms that we are *against* disarmament." The dizziest of war hawks would never allow himself to become responsible for a pronouncement like that. If he so much as put it into a draft, his press agent would explain that he was breaking the very first rule of war-hawkism, which is to write *"for"* where Goldwater has *"against."* Only after this is done would he be free to argue the case for more bombs, more bullets, more everything.

Some dim awareness of this basic rule must have led Goldwater to write his almost hysterical caveat, quoted above, at the end of *Why Not Victory?* But the damage cannot be undone in this fashion. Sentences like the one on disarmament are maximum-security cells, and the man who writes them or authorizes them has imprisoned himself and cannot talk his way out later on. For while the American electorate does not wish to see a politician immobilized by what he has said or done in the past, it does expect him somehow or other to square past and present, to

demonstrate that this or that policy is an application or fulfillment of this or that principle laid down in the past. How, having
declared an emphatic and unqualified, even italicized opposition to disarmament, could Goldwater possibly have voted for
last fall's Treaty of Moscow? In all likelihood, he would not have
voted for it under any circumstances. But if he had considered
it prudent to do so—if he had felt that in the year since the publication of *Why Not Victory?* changes had occurred which justified ratification of that particular treaty—he would have had to
explain not just a change of view on a single matter but the re-
jection of a fundamental principle which he had laid down.

It is at least conceivable that Goldwater would have welcomed
an opportunity to vote with the majority on the civil-rights bill.
He was eager, at the time the Senate voted, to be considered a
regular Republican, and he knew pretty well that he would be the
candidate and would run on a platform that would contain some
endorsement of what was certain by July to be the law. He had
taken his stand with the Southerners on cloture, and he knew
that further opposition was quixotic—in its impact on legislation, certainly, and probably in its impact on the election. He
might have contrived, as Everett Dirksen so nimbly did, to justify joining the consensus merely by citing the futility of standing
outside it. He could have appealed to an even nobler value—
national unity.

But for Goldwater the opportunity had been all but foreclosed
by Brent Bozell—or some other hand guided by the "guiding
hand"—in *The Conscience of a Conservative*. In that book,
Goldwater allowed himself to be committed to a states'-rights
position that Jefferson Davis could hardly have found acceptable. It is that the Tenth Amendment to the Constitution "recognizes the states' jurisdiction" in all matters not specifically
designated as federal somewhere in the text of the Constitution.

So much granted, it follows that the whole contemporary concept of "civil rights" is constitutionally invalid and there is only
"an imagined conflict" between states' rights and civil rights.
Thus, while "it may be just or wise or expedient for Negro chil-

dren to attend the same schools as white children . . . they do not have a civil right to do so." This is the case because "education is one of the powers reserved to the states by the Tenth Amendment." The reader of the Tenth Amendment will not find this to be the case. Education is a word—or a "power"—that is not mentioned in that amendment or anywhere else in the Constitution, which also omits any mention of outer space, radio and television, narcotics, child care, public accommodations, the right to work, trade unions, and Communism.

In turning over his intellectual franchise to Bozell and others, Goldwater has bound himself to a view of the Constitution that no President since Washington could have lived with. No major candidate in this century has so much as tried to live with anything like it—for the obvious reason that it denies the existence of almost every urgent problem of the age. "The Constitution," it is written in *The Conscience of a Conservative,* "is what its authors intended it to be and said it was—not what the Supreme Court says it is." And Goldwater has elsewhere said, "I believe in the Constitution of the United States as it was written one-hundred-and-eighty [*sic*] years ago and not as it is being 'interpreted' today." * This is not merely a fundamentalist or reactionary or unhistorical (his dating is off not by years but by centuries; part of the Constitution was "written" in A.D. 1964) or eccentric view, but a downright impossible one. It cannot be defended in rational discourse. For Goldwater to "believe" what he says he believes is to defy just about everything we know of language, logic, history, and law. It makes about as much sense as might be made by a man who says he likes food very much but is opposed to eating it. The Constitution is made of words, and words exist to be read, and to read is to "interpret," and Goldwater "interprets" every time he opens his mouth about

* If Bozell is responsible for the words or the concept, he has already retracted them. In the article "Freedom or Virtue?" his desire to uphold virtue over freedom compels him to argue that "It is a mistake to make demigods out of the framers or to read as a piece of scripture what they wrote."

the Constitution. This much at least he has in common with the Supreme Court. Impossible or not, the "belief" is still operative and binding on the candidate, who, on the eve of the Republican convention, told *Der Spiegel:* "I voted against [the civil-rights bill] on Constitutional grounds."

The Goldwater line on the Constitution has been tailored to fit his antifederalism. The fit is atrocious, but this seems a matter of small concern to him and to other politicians who for a number of reasons do not this year wish to acknowledge the existence of national problems. But Goldwater is—if we take him at his word—more, much more than an antifederalist. He doesn't want the federal power to dominate the states, but he does want it to dominate the world. And here the Constitution is not in the least inhibiting. "Our objective," he says in *Why Not Victory?,* "must be the destruction of the enemy as an ideological force and the removal of Communists from power wherever they hold it." He has lately hedged a bit as to the means, but he has at the same time expanded the ends. In the *Spiegel* interview, he said his aim would be "victory where our concepts of government, our concepts of freedom would replace the false concepts of communism [in this] struggle between godless people and the people of God." If his view of federal authority on this continent is unprecedentedly and impossibly narrow, his view of federal authority on other continents is unprecedentedly sweeping and on the face of it unconstitutional. If past Presidents had read their mandates in this way, the nation would have been perpetually at war, perpetually crusading, perpetually subjugating.

The antifederalist Goldwater would Balkanize the Union and thus diminish the power with which crusader Goldwater would threaten the "godless people." It would take a lot of divine assistance to make it work—even to have the country survive the attempt. The attempt is unlikely ever to be made, even in the unlikely event of Goldwater's election.

But a great party will nominate both the genial Arizona politician and the dour rightist ideologue; the two are fused now, and a factionalist—a profoundly nonpublic man—will come in at least second in November. This should cause a good many of us to re-examine our assumptions about the workings of the American party system. For in a most peculiar sense Goldwater owes his success to the widespread belief that the system was a machine constructed to produce a result opposite from the one about to be produced in San Francisco. All the Republican leaders of the era that has now closed—with the possible exception of Nelson Rockefeller—thought Goldwater's elimination inevitable. Their behavior—from Eisenhower's early commitment to neutrality, to Scranton's belated campaign—can only be explained in terms of their ideas of how the system should work. Because they thought it could not happen, it is happening.

PART TWO

Trial Heats and Finals

We have lost election after election in this country because conservative Republicans get mad and stay home.

—Goldwater, addressing delegates at the 1960 Republican National Convention

What would Goldwater do if he were President today? . . . What, specifically, would he have the government do? Here are his most "ultra" domestic proposals. He would: 1) Get the government out of agriculture and welfare—altogether. 2) Apply anti-monopoly legislation against the big labor unions. 3) Abolish the progressive income tax. In foreign affairs, he would: 1) Eliminate foreign aid except to nations actively prepared to assist in the anti-Communist enterprise. 2) Eliminate economic and cultural exchange programs, which he views as counterfeit considering the actual relationship between the Soviet Union and the United States. 3) Continue nuclear testing. And 4) "be prepared to undertake military programs against vulnerable Communist regimes" in the cause of pressing for victory against the Soviet Union. . . . Such a program is completely at odds with the programs adopted in 1960, by both the Democratic and the Republican parties. . . . Goldwater means it. If he had his way, the farmer's checks would stop coming in, the labor-union leader would face a law telling him he couldn't strike an entire industry, the businessman wouldn't get his cozy little tariff [?], the apartment dweller wouldn't have his rent frozen, the unemployed wouldn't get a federal check, nor the teacher federal money, nor the Little Rock Negroes their paratroops.

—William F. Buckley, Jr., editor of the *National Review*, in *Rumbles Left and Right*, 1963

The God who made New Hampshire
Taunted the lofty land
with little men.

> —Ralph Waldo Emerson, "Ode Inscribed to W. H. Channing," 1846

That word brinksmanship is a great word. . . . Have the people of New England [changed] in the last two hundred years? Have we become a nation of cowards? . . . I would like to suggest one change, that social security be voluntary.

> —Goldwater, in New Hampshire, as quoted in *Goldwater From A to Z,* by Arthur Frommer, Pocket Books, 1964

March 15, 1964

Ambassador Lodge has swept New Hampshire with thirty-three
thousand write-in votes, but he will stay on at his post in South
Vietnam through at least a few more primaries, and will thus remain bound by the Foreign Service regulations that prohibit an
officer from engaging in partisan controversy. Seldom, one imagines, has a prohibition been more welcome. Saigon is a privileged
sanctuary; the gag rule is emancipating. The losers in the New
Hampshire primary insist that Lodge owes it to the party and to
the country to come home and "debate the issues." What they
want is not controversy but company; they want Lodge to share
the perils of exposure and disclosure. Senator Goldwater, talking to some college students in California two days ago, said that
he thought it would be in the national interest to have Lodge address a joint session of Congress on the situation in South Vietnam. An interesting precedent would be established if this were
to happen, but it isn't likely to. The Ambassador today has no
more need to be advised by Senator Goldwater than Cassius
Clay has to receive instruction from Sonny Liston. The Ambassador may not keep the heavyweight Republican title for long,
but if and when it is taken from him, the loss will not be attributable to any flaws in his present strategy. Presidential politics is
unlike boxing in that it is entirely possible for a man to become
a champion in his division without ever climbing into the ring.
In 1952, the Democrats denied their nomination to the late Estes

Kefauver, who had fought for it all over the country and won a number of spectacular victories, and thrust it upon Adlai Stevenson, who had been deskbound in Springfield, Illinois, and occupied largely with telling people he didn't want to be a candidate. In the same year, Dwight Eisenhower, a noncombatant with a job in Paris, swept the New Hampshire Republican primary and remained abroad until a few weeks before the national convention. He returned in June—at the urging of his manager, Henry Cabot Lodge—to "campaign" against Robert A. Taft. He didn't "debate the issues," though. Instead, he made what he so accurately described in his recent volume of memoirs as "a series of personal appearances." These may have been helpful. Taft was a strong and resourceful opponent, and at the time of Eisenhower's return he had about 80 per cent of the delegates he needed to win nomination on the first ballot. Lodge is, of course, no Eisenhower, but neither is Goldwater a Taft, and in theory, at least, there is absolutely no reason for Lodge not to stand mute in Saigon until all the debaters have exhausted themselves and their audiences, and until all the tiresome primaries are over.

There are certain disadvantages in this strategy, but most of them seem rather easy to overcome, and the compensating advantages are large. It is said to be difficult to raise money for an absentee candidate, and no doubt it is. The shoppers like to see the merchandise. On the other hand, the present Lodge strategy doesn't call for much money. The government is paying all his bills in Saigon, and he doesn't have to charter any airplanes, trains, or buses; no stadiums have to be rented, and no large staff of researchers and ghost writers must be maintained. If there is any serious demand to know Lodge's "position" on any of the "issues," it can be satisfied in a number of ways. In a long public career, Lodge has addressed himself to just about every question of policy there is; it's all on the record in one form or another. Moreover, he has a son who seems not only a devoted follower and a shrewd organizer but an eloquent spokesman. On one matter, Lodge is free to speak as often as he wants. According to Goldwater, Rockefeller, and Nixon, the big Republican issue in 1964 will be "the fight against Communism." Lodge can't criticize President Johnson on this, but he isn't running against the President at the moment, and neither is anyone else. But he can join with the others in denouncing the Communists and all their works at the top of his voice any time he feels like it; in fact, this is one of the things the government is paying him to do. And his position in South Vietnam gives his supporters one enormous advantage. They can point out that while Goldwater and the others are merely *talking* about Communism in supermarket parking lots, their man is actually *doing* something about it right up in the front lines. One picture of Lodge surrounded by armed anti-Vietcong guerrillas in the Mekong Delta must be worth, even at a conservative's estimate, three of Barry Goldwater surrounded by anti-Castro banqueters in the Beverly Hilton.

In the event of any really urgent need to provide clarification or amplification, Lodge might adapt to his own purposes a device employed by the late Joseph R. McCarthy on the eve of his Senate career. In 1944, when McCarthy first sought the Republican nomination for the Senate, he was both a circuit judge on the Wisconsin Supreme Court and a captain in the United States Marines. Wisconsin law held that he could not, as a judge, run for any nonjudicial office, and military regulations forbade him to speak publicly on any political issues. McCarthy ignored the state law and got around the military regulations by coming home from the South Pacific on a thirty-day pass and telling voters what views he would express if he were free to express any views. For example, he began a speech to the Milwaukee League of Women Voters by saying, "I wish I could discuss the importance of oil and the importance of maintaining a strong Army and Navy. But I may not do so. If I were able to speak, here's what I'd say. . . ." He went on from there.

Lodge's showing in New Hampshire was a surprise even to those opinion-samplers who had canvassed the state and had expected him to do quite well. They do not think his victory can be explained as that of a "favorite son" or a "regional candidate." On the contrary, they see it as an outsider's triumph. Of the four leading candidates, Lodge was the only one who had no prominent New Hampshire politicians supporting him. All the established local politicians were on the ballot as delegates committed to one or another of the losers, and not one of them will be seated at the convention in July. New Hampshire has put Lodge in the running, and he will stay in it at least until the convention, for he has something of value to trade. He may have a good deal more to trade if General Eisenhower decides to endorse him. (It is believed that Eisenhower's prestige helped him mightily last week. While the Goldwater and Rockefeller forces were buying television time by the half hour, the Lodge people bought it by the half minute to show an old film clip of the General beaming at Lodge and saying, "This is the man we want. . . ." There must have been more to the sentence than that, but no one remembered the occasion, and there was no clue to what Eisenhower wanted Lodge *for.* Anyway, it was reported to be highly effective.) Thus far, Eisenhower has said nothing about the new situation created by the New Hampshire Republican voters. He is known, though, to look upon Lodge with admiration and gratitude; it is doubtful whether this could be said to be his view of any other candidate.

Despite Lodge's showing last week, and despite all the advantages his present position appears to give him, however, most people here feel that his chances of actually getting the nomination in July are slim. Wherever the political leaders are secure in their authority, Lodge will face hostility. He has never been well regarded in professional circles, and his troublemaking of last week will hardly improve his standing. Among those who still honor the memory of Robert Taft, Lodge is looked upon as an enemy commander. Many influential Republicans think he blew the 1960 election when he said that there ought to be a Negro in Richard Nixon's Cabinet. Conservative leaders recall with extreme distaste his role as Nikita Khrushchev's American cicerone in 1959, and they regard as an expression of almost treasonable sentiment his statement, made in the course of that memorable journey, that the United States could no longer be accurately described as a capitalist society. Most politicians who know him consider him starchy, sniffish, snobbish, and Bostonian to a quite unacceptable degree. No one up to now has ever thought highly of him as a campaigner. The elections he has won were all sure things. He was Eisenhower's campaign manager in 1952, but Eisenhower could not have lost in 1952 even if he had put Harold Stassen in charge of his affairs. While Eisenhower carried Massachusetts by two hundred thousand votes, Lodge lost his Senate seat to John F. Kennedy by seventy thousand. His service thereafter was in the United Nations, which is strictly extraterritorial as far as politicians are concerned; there are very few votes there, and the patronage is negligible. In professional circles, the impression is widespread that Lodge is wanting in diligence. There are ugly rumors to the effect that he is addicted to long afternoon naps—a practice considered winning in Calvin Coolidge and advisable for Lyndon Johnson but one that, in these stern times when Republican votes come hard, is evidently as inexcusable for a Republican as divorce.

Outside the camps of the hot partisans, the general view is that New Hampshire has strengthened the arguments of those who have been saying all along that the nomination of as militant a rightist as Goldwater would be fatal because of the votes it would cost in the industrial states. New Hampshire seems to have exposed as groundless the political assumption upon which right-wing Republicans have been basing their claims to recognition for the past quarter century. From Taft's quest for the nomination in 1940 to Goldwater's in 1964, the argument has been that the United States is a basically conservative country and that the reason so many people don't vote in primary or general elections is that the conservative masses see no point in troubling to express their preference for one liberal over another liberal. But if these people exist anywhere, they don't seem to exist in New Hampshire, and it is hard to see how the Taft-Goldwater theory can be upheld after an election that set a widely publicized rightist against the field and gave the rightist less than one vote in four. It is axiomatic that no Republican can win a national election unless he can poll just about the full strength of his own party and, as Eisenhower did, attract millions of non-Republican voters as well. In New Hampshire, every vote that Goldwater didn't get was a vote against him, and the tabulations seem to cast considerable doubt on whether the Senator could count on carrying his own party—outside the South, which is a special case and not an important one at this stage— if he should be the candidate on November 3.

A Republican of the Lodge-Rockefeller persuasion would almost certainly lose the party the votes of many of those who turned out for Goldwater last week, but the numbers would matter little, since there would be the hope of more than making up for the loss by attracting independent and Democratic support. Nevertheless, the feeling here is that the party would also be risking its whole future if it nominated anyone whom the Goldwater people could not in good conscience support. For while it now seems plainly a myth that there are tens of millions of citizens waiting for a chance to support a true rightist, there is no doubt at all that there are a good many thousand Republicans who are passionate in their rightist convictions and who are terribly bitter over what they regard as the shameful treatment accorded their spokesmen throughout the years since 1940. They are people who are willing to work hard and to give of their wealth, which is in many cases considerable, for a leader who represents them as Goldwater does. In recent years, thanks largely to Goldwater's gift for firing their enthusiasm and mobilizing their energies, they have managed to win effective control of many pieces of political machinery. They are firmly in charge of the party not only throughout most of the South but in large areas west of the Mississippi. The Republican organization in Texas is theirs and theirs alone, and it is powerful enough to have sent to Congress two men—Senator John Tower and Representative Bruce Alger—who have contrived to occupy ground well to the right of Barry Goldwater's. Even in New Hampshire, the right wing controlled, until last week, most of the machinery. The Goldwater faction has been strong in the National Committee, whose chairman, Representative William E. Miller, of New York, generally sounds as if his own sympathies were deeply engaged by rightist candidates and rightist doctrines.

It will be argued by Goldwater's rivals from the East that the consequences of giving offense to the rightists would not be terribly grave. They can point to 1952, when the national convention rejected Taft for the fourth and last time. There was no serious trouble; the party prospered greatly, and Eisenhower brought Goldwater in on his coattails. Where else, the Republican liberals are sure to say, can the conservatives go? But the situation in 1952 was very different from the situation in 1964. Eisenhower was the candidate of the liberals, but he was never really one of their number; he was in many ways to the right of Taft. Besides, he was a great presence in American life, and his willingness to serve the Republicans was practically an assurance of their return to power. No one in the field today could bring to the party more than a fraction of the strength that Eisenhower brought to it. The prospect seems to be for defeat no matter who runs.

It is the contempt Goldwater has shown for the leadership that has attracted the larger part of his following. He is by temperament anything but a fanatic himself, but the fanatics have been drawn to him. His principal financial backers differ in many ways from those who supported Taft. Taft drew much of his support from Middle Western industrialists and bankers who had some understanding of the imperatives of an industrial society; they didn't spend much time denouncing the graduated income tax or Social Security. Goldwater's support comes largely from Southwestern speculators and promoters whose economic views and practices are largely pre-industrial. They have no tradition of Republicanism; many of them are former Democrats, and their loyalty is not to the Republican Party but to Goldwater and Goldwaterism.

backlash, n. A sudden and violent movement backward, as the recoil of waves.

—Webster's New International Dictionary

Governor George C. Wallace of Alabama polled 34.1 percent of the Democratic votes cast in the Wisconsin presidential primary held yesterday [April 7]. . . . In the Indiana voting [May 5], Governor Wallace attracted 29.8 of the Democratic votes.

—Newspaper accounts

* WHITES WHA' HAE WI' WALLACE BLED:
A LETTER FROM WASHINGTON

May 8, 1964

All politics seem at the moment topsy-turvy. In Ohio, a man named Kennedy came close to winning a Democratic congressional nomination, partly, it is said, on the strength of the name he proudly bore and traded upon, partly on the strength of his record as a militant, articulate white supremacist. He died while the returns were still coming in. In the Indiana Democratic primary, Governor George C. Wallace, of Alabama, was the favorite of the industrial proletariat of Lake County, who also nominated a Negro for one local office and a prominent white integrationist for another. Senator Goldwater keeps slipping in popular support while gaining convention delegates. Dr. Gallup's latest soundings show Goldwater favored by 14 per cent of his party's rank and file, as against Ambassador Lodge's 37 per cent and Richard Nixon's 28. Harold Stassen was stronger in Indiana than Goldwater is in the entire country. Yet it now seems that Goldwater will go to the Republican convention only about ninety votes short of the six hundred and fifty-five needed for nomination. If he defeats Governor Rockefeller in California next month, he will be only four short of the magic number, and it will be extremely difficult for the convention to deny the nomination to a candidate favored by one out of every seven party voters.

All things considered, Goldwater has been doing extraordinarily well. If he doesn't get the nomination, he will be in a position to decide which of his rivals will get it. However, a conclusion that might be drawn from recent polls, official and unofficial, is that if Goldwater is serious about the Presidency and about his rightist convictions, he really ought to be a Democrat. It is a bit late for him to do anything about this in 1964, but it is something he might be thinking about for 1968 or 1972. His appeal, according to Governor Rockefeller and others who oppose him, is primarily to the "extremists" in the Republican Party. This is said to be even truer of Governor Wallace in the Democratic Party. Yet in Democratic primaries in two large and reasonably representative Northern states—Wisconsin and Indiana—Wallace has attracted more than 30 per cent of the votes. And he may do a good deal better than that in Maryland ten days from now. Apparently, there are many more Democratic than Republican extremists, even if due allowance is made for Republican "crossovers," and, as a matter of record, there are many more Democrats than Republicans. Indeed, one statistician here, extrapolating Wallace's primary showings, the numerical superiority of Democrats to Republicans across the country, and the prevalence of segregationist and states'-rights views in the South, has estimated that there are more Democratic extremists than there are Republicans of all varieties. Among Northern Democrats, Wallace labors under many disadvantages that would not encumber Goldwater if he switched over. Wallace is an Alabama carpetbagger bent on mischief and ready for insurrection, in which he has already had some experience. He breathes rancor, his manner is at once cold and abrasive, and his speech is an assault on the central nervous system. But what he has been advocating up North is just about indistinguishable from what Goldwater has been advocating North, South, East, and West. (Senator Goldwater is not a white supremacist, as Wallace is, but Wallace has not been addressing himself directly to the race question in his Northern appearances.) Where Wallace offends, Goldwater charms. He is innocent of rancor and about as abrasive as a jar of cold cream. He may appeal to extremists, and he may even be one, but he doesn't look or sound like one. If he had chosen the right party to begin with, he would, one imagines, be running a lot stronger than Wallace, whose arrogance and virulence and contempt for the law must put off a lot of voters. Goldwater is modest and gentle, and has never been a sit-in or stand-in demonstrator as Wallace was in Tuscaloosa last year. Goldwater is also much better known than Wallace. As a Democrat, he should be able to hold the extremist 30 to 35 per cent of the party and draw support from other factions. As a states'-rights Democrat, rather than a right-to-work Republican, he might find support in one section of the populace that up to now has shown nothing but hostility toward him—organized labor. Though Wallace has also offended the unions by supporting right-to-work laws, he swept some working-class districts in Gary and Hammond with as much as 65 per cent of the vote.

Civil-rights proponents in both parties here are making all kinds of efforts to explain away the Wallace vote. Some, like Senator Humphrey, say that the only important thing about Wallace's candidacy is that it has thus far met with defeat. These people point out that his Wisconsin and Indiana opponents got two-thirds of the party vote, which, they say with unquestionable accuracy, is a very large margin of victory in any political contest in this country. Others say that the primaries in Wisconsin and Indiana are not to be taken seriously, because in neither case was Wallace running against a serious candidate for the Presidency. Governors John W. Reynolds and Matthew E. Welsh had their names put on the ballot only to oppose Wallace and to make sure that regular party men will be seated as delegates in Atlantic City in August. In Maryland, week after next, Senator Daniel B. Brewster will provide the opposition for the same reasons. It is said that if President Johnson's name were on the ballot in any of the states in which Wallace is campaigning, the vote for Wallace would be negligible—perhaps 10 per cent. (In other words, two-thirds of the extremists would vote for Johnson.) Another argument is that the absence of the President's name or that of any other national figure turns the primaries into referendums on local issues. Thus, in Wisconsin and Indiana it was the performances of the two governors that were being judged, and both governors were vulnerable. Organization Democrats in Indiana say that the Wallace vote was essentially a protest against a new 2-per-cent sales tax that Governor Welsh supported. In a television interview two days ago, Senator Brewster managed to discount one-third of the Wallace vote by saying that 10 per cent of the voters are permanently aggrieved and can be counted upon in any election to support "any nameless, faceless man" who is represented to them as being in total opposition to established local or national authority. The same day, the President, in his family-style news conference, resorted to the now familiar device of figuring the extremist candidate's percentage of the total Presidential preference vote in both parties and suggesting that this is the true measure of his strength. By this means, the President brought Wallace down to 20 per cent (actually, it would be about 18), and said he hardly regarded this as an "overwhelming endorsement." If he had combined this approach with that of Senator Brewster on the chronic naysayers, the percentage could have been cut to a rather encouraging 8 or 10.

Certain military and geopolitical strategists have from time to time come up with figures on the number of deaths that a society like ours might regard as "acceptable" in the first stages of thermonuclear war. By "acceptable" they mean "endurable." The figures always seem fairly high. As far as is known, the social sciences have not advanced to the point of estimating how much bigotry or how widespread a response to demagogy a free and normally peaceable society can endure. Certainly the figure must be above 30 per cent; conceivably it could be above 50 per cent. Almost on the eve of his downfall ten years ago, Senator McCarthy, according to the polls, was held in good opinion by exactly half the country. But despite the current efforts of the liberals to discount the Wallace showing, the fact is that there are few, if any, of them who have not been astonished and dismayed by his showing. None of them can point to a forecast of anything like so large a vote for him; he himself said he would "rattle the eyeteeth" of the liberals if he got 15 per cent in Wisconsin, and that was probably an honest estimate of what he expected. Nor, a couple of months back, was anyone explaining that support of a racist in a Presidential primary wouldn't really have much to do with racism, that it would most likely reflect a concern with local issues like sales taxes, or that a large part of it would be attributable to pure cussedness. The fact that the interpretations were not offered in advance of the events does not invalidate them. Some believers in racial equality and brotherhood may have voted for Wallace because they thought he had the better of the argument over the relationship between the federal government and the states. Many, one can be almost certain, would not have voted for him if they had thought his candidacy a real threat to President Johnson's. None of this diminishes the size of the vote that he actually got, or what appears to be its simplest meaning—freely given approval, on a secret ballot, of a man primarily known as a believer in segregation, a doctrine he would carry to the point of denying training in his state university to a single qualified Negro. In many ways, a vote in a primary election has a significance larger than that of a vote in a general election. It is, as the right-wing publicist William F. Buckley, Jr., noted in a celebration of Wallace's showing in Wisconsin, "an act of considerable decisiveness." Except for those who are economically dependent on politics—government employees and their families—voters in primaries are expressing conviction beyond the conventional call of civic virtue. There are high-minded campaigns to get people out to "vote for the party of their choice," but very few to get them to vote *in* their parties.

The President and others may say that a 20- or 30-per-cent vote for Wallace is nothing to get alarmed about, nothing to make the teeth rattle. But there would be a deafening rattle of teeth if ever there were a 30-per-cent vote—or a 20- or a 10-per-cent vote—for a *Communist* candidate in either a general election or a primary election, or even in the most unreliable straw poll. J. Edgar Hoover would submit an FBI budget at least as large as that of the Defense Department. Congressmen would be trampling one another in the rush to get antisedition bills into the legislative hopper. The "issue" that would thus be created would displace all others. There might be slightly less havoc if a spokesman for a *black*-supremacy movement made as much political headway among Negroes as Wallace evidently has among whites, but there would be havoc enough. The most striking thing about the Wallace performance is, of course, the performance itself. But the next most striking thing is that it really hasn't caused much alarm and appears unlikely to have much of an impact on events. This, too, is a surprise. It had been clear for months that the increased militancy of the Negro organizations and the agitation to codify and establish by statute those "rights" that the courts hold are already part of the law (all the current legislation is really aimed at the elimination of civil "wrongs") would breed resistance in the North as well as in the South. Not many people thought in terms of a large primary vote for Governor Wallace, but quite a few supposed that congressmen from Northern cities and suburban districts would get a bit edgy when they learned that many white plumbers didn't look forward to working side by side with Negro plumbers and that homeowners might come down on the wrong side when property values and human values were in conflict. The nonce word for this was "backlash," and it was feared that it would endanger the civil-rights bill to which President Kennedy gave the highest legislative priority last June. The late President and his brother were so fearful of this backlash that they pleaded with the liberal leadership in Congress not to send to the floor as strong a bill as the one it did eventually propose. On the evidence thus far available, these particular fears were groundless. Most of the expected reactions in time materialized, but a strong bill passed the House with ease and, despite Governor Wallace, is expected to pass the Senate more or less intact. If it should fail in the Senate, it will be not because of the backlash or because of Governor Wallace but because the rules under which the Senate operates make it difficult for even a substantial majority to prevail.

The size of the Wallace vote has shocked and surprised most people here, which may demonstrate how far out of touch with reality Washington may be. On the other hand, the reaction may demonstrate a kind of political sophistication that many thought was lacking in this community. It is a serious problem for any society when disaffection rises to the point where 20 or 30 per cent of the people (there is really not much reason to suppose that bigotry and racial hatred are less widespread in the population as a whole than among Democratic voters) will lend their support to a subversive figure. But there is plenty of evidence that sound policy and prudent leadership can deal with problems of this sort. For reasons that have to do with our whole history and outlook, we would almost certainly become badly unstrung if there were suddenly a sizable Bolshevik movement; our years of isolation and inviolable nationalism have given us a particular horror of movements led by or associated with foreigners. But several free and flourishing societies in Europe have survived long periods when Communist blocs commanded the loyalty of at least as many people as might be inclined to support Governor Wallace. The test is whether a large minority can so unsettle a majority or its leaders as to deflect the majority from its purposes. Thus far, nothing of the sort seems to be happening here. The civil-rights bill is not yet sure of passage, but it is closer to it than anyone thought it would be at the beginning of the year.

The Wallace vote remains a fact of certain significance, even though it is of uncertain consequence and perhaps of no direct political consequence. It cannot be stripped of all unpleasantness and made a mere expression of pique, eccentricity, or generalized political frustration. It was a large vote for a man who stands for an ugly doctrine, even if he does not proclaim it in every speech, and it may somehow increase the prospects for racial violence in the months and years ahead. It says something about the nature and force of bigotry in this period, however, that the most impressive demonstration of it has been made in a *vote*, on ballots marked by individuals. There is in the North no party of bigotry, and no organized bigot faction in either party. As far as is known, the organized groups outside the parties are feeble and are themselves torn by factionalism. And there is the topsy-turviness of the whole situation, which can lead some people to vote for a segregationist on one line and an integrationist on another, to favor a man because he is named Kennedy and because he is opposed to most of what the name is generally understood to imply. The bigotry exists and is alarming, but it seems a bit short of obsessive. If it can be released and contained in the voting booth, it can be endured, and we can count ourselves lucky.

I have refused to join "stop-Goldwater," "stop-Rockefeller," or "stop-anybody" movements.

—William W. Scranton, Governor of Pennsylvania, on the eve of the California primary

The final tally was: Goldwater, 1,089,892 (51.4 per cent); Rockefeller, 1,031,661 (48.6 per cent).

—California primary returns, June 2, 1964

* BIG DEAL IN CALIFORNIA: A LETTER FROM WASHINGTON

June 5, 1964

Senator Goldwater has carried California, and the established oracles here are deep in their caves—in some cases sharing space with chagrined and weary computers—and are muttering prophecies laced with "if"s, "but"s, and "on the other hand"s. They seem to be saying that after California Senator Goldwater cannot be denied the nomination, and that he cannot be given it, either. Any appeal to precedent is useless. No candidate in modern times has gone to a convention with more than five hundred delegates and left without the nomination. Nor has any candidate been chosen who placed second or lower in rank-and-file support, as both the official and the unofficial polls have measured it. Goldwater will have five hundred delegates and then some, but against organized opposition he has come in first only in California—or, to be a bit more precise, in Los Angeles and its immediate environs. History will simply have to be made at the Republican convention next month. It must disregard either its own members—the delegates, that is—or the party rank and file; it cannot satisfy both. Conventions have been known to take the people's choice over the delegates' preference. Robert A. Taft was the man the delegates liked in 1952, but General Eisenhower was the man they chose, because they had become persuaded that the country liked him. But this convention will not be able to follow that example, for today there is no people's choice. There is no Eisenhower, not even a Willkie.

There is no front-runner—only Senator Goldwater, who invariably comes in ahead of Senator Margaret Chase Smith and Harold Stassen in public-opinion polls but finishes well behind Ambassador Lodge, Richard Nixon, and Governor Rockefeller, the last three running sometimes in that order, sometimes in another. If the convention accepts Goldwater, as it now seems almost bound to do, it will be breaking with more than one tradition.

Goldwater looks unstoppable, but a stop-Goldwater movement exists, even after California. It is feeble and leaderless—feeble *because* it is leaderless—but it is not quite hopeless. It gets what nourishment it can from two hopes. One is that General Eisenhower, as he thinks things over in the next few days, will come to see in Goldwater's ascendancy an affront to his own record (once described by Goldwater as a "dime-store New Deal") and to his own brand of conservatism. The other is that Goldwater will do or say something (conceivably in the course of next week's civil-rights maneuverings in the Senate) that will stiffen resistance wherever resistance is still to be found. The movement is sustained by two arguments, or conclusions, that are unaffected by the results in California. The first is that Goldwater would be a drag on the ticket in all but a handful of states, none of which is of much importance in terms of electoral votes. The second is that his candidacy would put control of Republican Party machinery in the hands of right-wing zealots who are irregular Republicans at best and who care less about such enduring values as votes, harmony, and patronage than about what they regard as sound doctrine on fluoridation, Castro, and the House Committee on Un-American Activities. The first argument has more demonstrable merit than the second. The opinion polls have lost some of their prestige by their failure to name the winners in this spring's trial heats, but they have not been wrong by more than two or three percentage points, and they have spotted the major trends even when they have not properly gauged their force. In their estimates of how Goldwater is running in the country at large, they could be in error by ten or fifteen points and still leave him a sure loser in the election. At the moment, it would seem, a staggering majority of voters see Goldwater as a man made of some lighter, less durable wood than Presidential timber. (One recent poll showed 40 per cent of Republicans throughout the nation favoring President Johnson over both Rockefeller and Goldwater.) The Goldwater people can counter, 'of course, by pointing out that no other Republican seems to have captured the affection of the general public this year, and that if Republican moderates and liberals prefer Johnson to Rockefeller, then their man would not do appreciably worse, and might even do better, in electoral votes than anyone else. As far as the Presidency is concerned, the logic is sound enough, but party leaders in the large Eastern and Midwestern states have a good deal more on their minds than the Presidency and the Electoral College. What troubles them about Goldwater is the damage they think he might do to the rest of their tickets.

It is this concern with the grubbier and more parochial aspects of the election that has bred heavy—though disorganized—resistance to Goldwater in every industrial state. In some cases, ideology has played a part, in some it has not. Men like Senators Thomas H. Kuchel, in California, and Javits, in New York, would no doubt have felt obliged to oppose Goldwater even if they thought he would bring strength rather than weakness to the party as a whole. With others, the case is different. In Ohio, the governor, James Rhodes, and the state chairman, Ray Bliss, are men who by temperament and conviction—though not by proclamation—are fully as conservative as Goldwater, yet they are as apprehensive about Goldwater's candidacy as any of the other state leaders. They preside over one of the most successful Republican organizations in the country; they wish to hold their power in the state this year and extend their power in Washington by winning for Robert A. Taft, Jr., the Senate seat his conservative father once occupied. On this account, they have held back from the movement into which their political sympathies might in other circumstances have led them, and there is every reason to suppose that they would give aid and comfort to any effort to stop Goldwater that seemed to have a good chance of success.

Their position illustrates the strength of the argument that Goldwater would damage the ticket and the weakness of the argument that his candidacy would give him and his followers control of the party machinery, thereby insuring the destruction of the Republican Party as we know it—a dark view that appeals to editorial writers and to those charged with writing anti-Goldwater speeches and press releases. Goldwater's influence is a divisive one (though, as Nixon said the other day, a successful effort to stop him might be even more divisive), and in nominating him the party would run a strong risk of losing other offices while failing to gain the Presidency. But the notion that if Goldwater runs and loses this year, his followers will nevertheless win control of the party will not stand up under close scrutiny. Nationally, there is hardly any party machinery, Republican or Democratic, to control. There are only the National Committees, which in defeat have little to do but dodge bill collectors and in victory become the tools of the White House. If it were otherwise, Nixon would be in charge of the Republican Party machinery today, and the candidate would be a man he favored—probably himself. As for the state organizations, it is evident that Goldwater people have for some time been in control of many of them. This is what makes Goldwater a serious candidate. In the event that he is nominated in July and defeated in November, he and his supporters will have less authority than they have right now—exactly as Nixon and his supporters have far less authority now than they had four years ago. From the viewpoint of those who are persuaded that Goldwater could not possibly win the election, there could be no surer way of driving him and his friends from party power than by giving him the nomination. After November, most of the power would pass from those who had encouraged his candidacy to those who had opposed it, and in particular to those Republican politicians, if any, who had won while he lost.

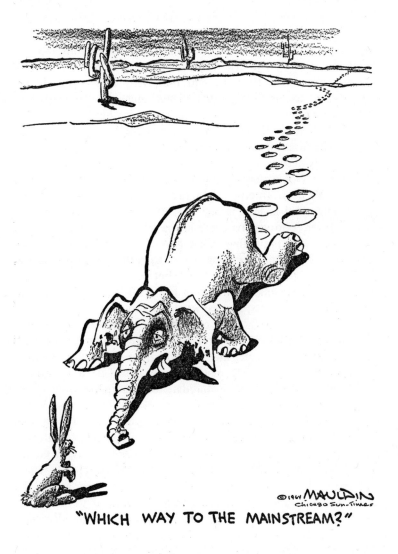

"WHICH WAY TO THE MAINSTREAM?"

This shift of power would occur even if men like Robert Taft, Jr., and Charles H. Percy, the Chicago businessman who is running as a Republican moderate for governor of Illinois, went down to defeat with Goldwater and unmistakably because of Goldwater. It is the fear that public offices will be lost to Democrats, rather than the fear that party leadership will be transferred to the Goldwater radicals, that will give the stop-Goldwater movement whatever strength it may have in San Francisco next month. It cannot have much strength without a leader, and at the moment none is in sight. Scranton and Nixon are the only two who seem to have a chance of rallying enough support to threaten Goldwater, but neither of them appears to want any part of such an enterprise. In fact, the only movement they seem interested in now is one to stop the stoppers. If General Eisenhower, who was reported in the Washington *Post* the day after the California voting as being in a "foul mood," wished to intervene, he might prevail on one or the other of them to come to the aid of the party he once led, but he made what he seems to regard as his final contribution last week when he said, in a statement to the press, that he would like to see the party nominate a man bearing a close resemblance to himself. If no one can recruit Scranton or Nixon, the anti-Goldwater people will have to suffer Goldwater and try to restrain him by forcing him to stand on a moderate platform and alongside a liberal or moderate Vice-Presidential candidate. Such an effort would provide an interesting, if unedifying, spectacle. Goldwater doesn't want any platform this year—and one can see why. Of the twenty-five major provisions of the 1960 Republican platform, according to a recent analysis made by Senator Javits, Goldwater has since taken a stand, in votes or in speeches, against all twenty-five. A platform will be adopted this year, and while it is inconceivable that a convention determined to nominate Goldwater would saddle him with policies that he could accept only by repudiating his entire past, it is hard to see, in view of the record, how it could write a platform acceptable to him without repudiating the Republican Party's recent past. It is

equally hard to see how a Republican ticket with Goldwater at
its head could possibly be "balanced." Every name thus far
mentioned has been that of a man committed to policies Goldwater has opposed—on civil rights, on nuclear testing, on almost the whole range of domestic and foreign affairs. Someone
—perhaps everyone—is going to have to rise above principle.
In Goldwater's case, the price might be a great diminution of
enthusiasm for him on the far-right flank of the party, where
the tendency to expect foul betrayal is rather strong and is often
accompanied by downright enjoyment of it. It is a price that
many Republicans would be delighted to have him pay.

The prospect of a Johnson-Goldwater election this fall dismays
Republicans and Democrats here in approximately equal numbers, and for what may be described as generally bipartisan
reasons. It is the probable character of the autumn campaign,
rather than its probable outcome, that is disturbing. For Goldwater's candidacy would almost certainly mean that the debate
would turn on issues that have, for good or ill, long since been
settled by history. As an instance, it may have been—as Goldwater believes it was—a mistake for the United States to recognize the Soviet Union in 1933. But the mistake, if that is what
it was, is a matter to be dealt with today not by politicians but
by historians, for it is recorded in the archives that diplomatic
relations were established in that year, and the serious political
question thirty-one years later (and far more than thirty-one
bilateral and multilateral treaties and other agreements later) is
not whether diplomatic relations are to be continued but how
they are to be conducted—what the nature and terms and purposes of the established relations ought to be. Goldwater's view
until very recently was that recognition should be withdrawn.
This could, to be sure, be done with a stroke of the Presidential
pen—which would immediately have to be pressed into service
for the writing of an entirely new American foreign policy in
every part of the world. Goldwater has lately been saying that he
would not be in any particular hurry to withdraw recognition.
"That withdrawal," according to a manual recently circulated

by Goldwater headquarters, "might not come this year or next or at all." The Senator's present position, it is explained in this reassuring document, is that the "possibility" of withdrawal "should be held as a sword over the head of the Kremlin clique." It is probable that Goldwater will back away from, or waffle around, even this position as he approaches responsibility for his party's policies. But as far as the 1964 campaign is concerned, he will, even if he prefers not to, defend his past positions as well as his present ones. The Democrats, who enter elections in order to win them, will debate the Goldwater of their choosing—the most vulnerable one they can find.

There is in American politics something like a statute of limitations on past error, miscalculation, and heresy. It is based partly on political decency as codified in the understandings of the various politicians' guilds, partly on the fact that the memory of the electorate is short and that it is often hard to explain what was unpardonable about an act committed a good many years ago. In most cases, the term of the statute is approximately that of the Presidency, and it seldom happens that a man is held liable for anything he did or said more than four or five years ago. Goldwater was one of Senator McCarthy's stoutest defenders, and opposed the Senate's censure of McCarthy in 1954. No one is likely to make much of this in 1964. At one time, he favored outright repeal of the graduated income tax, but his position in recent years has been that this was merely a utopian vision and that he is not really a utopian. It would be surprising if he were not taken at his most recent word on matters of this sort. But even if he is compelled to modify or disown all those stated opinions that have led his adversaries to describe him as an extremist, he will be charged with many of them if he becomes his party's candidate. For it was not several years ago but within the past twelve months or so, during which he has been actively seeking the nomination, that he has proposed the severance of relations with the Soviet Union, the abandonment of the "peacekeeping and peacemaking" machinery of the United Nations, the mounting of a Marine invasion of Cuba from the Guantánamo base, the sale of the Tennessee Valley Authority, and the conversion of the Social Security system into a voluntary insurance plan. In the California campaign, he sought to avoid being held to account for these positions, but Rockefeller wouldn't allow it, and neither would President Johnson. (In all likelihood, the President himself will choose to stand on his Presidential dignity and discuss only his own views of the national interest and the general welfare. He will do so, though, only if he is confident that a host of lesser Democrats is acquainting the public with the more eccentric and extravagant of Goldwater's views and recommendations.) Moreover, it is hardly likely that Goldwater will alter the really fundamental concepts of foreign and domestic affairs that have given him his peculiar identity in American politics, setting him apart from all the other responsible leaders of both parties over the past few decades. It has been at least a quarter of a century since any national leader has maintained that our major social and economic problems were anything less than national in scope. Southern politicians have used the states'-rights argument to fight off federal policies they do not welcome, but even they are now finding it convenient to point out that civil rights are a national problem, and they have never maintained that the solution of serious economic questions can be arrived at by any authority but the federal one. Goldwater recognizes no national problems and no national responsibilities except those of foreign policy, defense, and the currency system. In foreign and defense policy, he is committed to the acceptance of an American mission that all national leaders in recent years have regarded as beyond our military, diplomatic, and moral means—"the removal of Communists from power wherever they hold it."

"You are the salt of the earth," Senator Carl T. Curtis, of Nebraska, the Goldwater floor leader, shouted to the delegates as he opposed the rules change. The answering roar showed that most of the audience thought he meant their kind of Republicans—not the "Eastern liberals."

—Anthony Lewis, in the New York *Times,* July 14, 1964

Anyone who joins us in all sincerity, we welcome. Those who do not care for our cause we do not expect to enter our ranks in any case.

And let our Republicanism, so focused and dedicated, not be made fuzzy and futile by unthinking and stupid labels. *I would remind you that extremism in the defense of liberty is no vice. And let me remind you that moderation in the pursuit of justice is no virtue.*

—Goldwater's acceptance speech, July 16, 1964. Italics his. "I like that," he is said to have said, upon coming on this passage, with a delight akin to that of Keats upon reading Chapman's Homer. The italicized sentences are reliably reported to have come from Karl Hess, his principal speech writer. Research on Hess's earlier writing turned up several other nifties. For example, in the *American Mercury* for May 1954 the following: "The question of freedom, when stripped to its steel center, is just this: Who has the guns? . . . It would not be America, really, if it did not produce men who suddenly tire of palaver and reach for the rifle on the wall. . . ."

✳ DEATH IN THE COW PALACE: A LETTER FROM SAN FRANCISCO

July 18, 1964

The platform adopted in the Cow Palace states that "within our republic the federal government should act only where it has constitutional authority to act." This is bipartisan, all-American doctrine; no one favors the contrary proposition. Between the parties and within them, there is on occasion some dispute as to what the limitations are; it can be a vexed question, even for learned judges. It gives Senator Goldwater little trouble, though, for he is a Constitutional fundamentalist. It is his belief, for example, that because "education" is a word nowhere to be found in the Constitution, it follows that "education is one of the powers reserved to the states." It therefore came as a distinct surprise when he announced that he would make an issue of crime and violence in the streets, parks, and transit systems of "our great cities." That the problem is grave and is nationwide in scope no one would deny. Until this week, though, no one had suggested federal responsibility or intervention except in places—most notably in certain parts of the deep South—where it was clear that local authorities lacked not the power, but the intention to protect certain citizens going peacefully about their business and where, very often, the authorities have themselves menaced lives, limbs, and property. But neither Goldwater nor anyone else who in the last few days has spoken with anxiety about terror and disorder in public and private places seems to have had these situations in mind, and it is certainly fair to conclude from the Republican candidate's record that he would agree with the Democratic Attorney General that the federal government is severely limited in its capacity and in its legal powers to provide safe passage to American citizens abroad or at home in, say, Mississippi. This sort of thing, Goldwater has said time and again, is the proper concern only of the states and of their political subdivisions. He is now, though, filled with a sense of urgency about some ugly situations in the great urban centers—he has thus far named only New York. In a press conference held the morning after his nomination, the Republican candidate put the agony of the cities second in importance only to foreign policy as an issue in his campaign against the present administration, and he astonished some of those present by saying, "I think the responsibility for this has to start some place, and it should start at the federal level with the federal courts enforcing the law." What law he had in mind he did not say, nor did he explain what Presidential powers he thought might be invoked, but in any case, he went on to say that "as President, I'm going to do all I can to see that women can go out in the streets of this country without being scared stiff."

The origin of this commendable but somewhat novel resolve is not clear. Goldwater exegetes say that it has never been a theme in his earlier writings and speeches. There were intimations of it in the platform—talk of "moral decline and drift" and an indictment of the Johnson administration for "encouraging disorderly and lawless elements"—but a national remedy is not among the many good things the platform promises. It was General Eisenhower who first brought the matter before the convention. In his address to the delegates—shortly after he had set them to stomping and screaming by expressing his displeasure with the press*—he said he wished to say "a word about an obligation that rests with special force upon the Republican party." He had several words, and the burden of them

* "So let us particularly scorn the divisive efforts of those outside our family, including sensation-seeking columnists and commentators, because,

was that the responsible Republican citizen was a man willing
to "help our governors, our mayors, and the organizations
operating under them to keep the peace and maintain order."
He stopped far short of making a federal case of the need for
better lighting and more policemen in the cities, but his mention
of these matters and of "the criminal . . . roaming the streets
with the switchblade knife" stirred the convention only slightly
less than his strictures on the press, and within thirty-six hours
Goldwater, the first states'-rights candidate in Republican history, had found a brand-new "responsibility" to be dealt with
"at the federal level." In his acceptance speech, delivered a few
hours after his first press conference as his party's candidate,
"violence in our streets" was again the number-two issue. It
came hard on the heels of "the wall of shame in Berlin, [and]
the sands of shame at the Bay of Pigs, [and] the slow death of
freedom in Laos." The Cow Palace rocked and trembled again.
One hoped the structure would be safe for the Beatles, who are
due here soon.

Wherever the new line originated, it was first tested here, this
last week, and the results were as gratifying to some as they
were appalling to others. The delegates and the galleries cheered
it with all the joy they put into their booing of Rockefeller.
None of the anti-Goldwater people seemed to find any grounds
on which they could criticize it. The press reaction is reported
to have been largely favorable. And for Goldwater himself it was
plainly a deliverance. He is not himself a racist, not a segregationist, and he opposed the civil-rights bill, he explained, only
because he regarded two sections of it as a usurpation of the
powers of the states. He has repeatedly said that he hopes that
questions of race can be kept out of the campaign, and he has
freely acknowledged that his own nomination is the principal
spur to their introduction. But he got where he is today because
segregationist politicians discounted as either false or irrelevant
his egalitarian professions and found most pleasing his views

---

my friends, I assure you, that these are people who couldn't care less
about the good of our party."

on all substantive political issues. He wants to hold these people and draw enough more of their kind to carry the South. He has said that he does not want what has become known as the "white backlash" vote outside the South. This is as yet a kind of phantom. No one is sure of its size or shape, no one knows quite where to find it. Something was learned about it in the vote for Governor Wallace in the Wisconsin, Indiana, and Maryland primaries, but offices were not changing hands in those contests, and it remains to be seen whether many voters will abandon their traditional habits and loyalties and concern for their pocketbooks in a general election and cast their votes for President on the basis of race. In any event, most politicians—Republicans and Democrats alike—know that it exists and hope or fear, as the case may be, that it is very large indeed. Among the hopers are the majority of the delegates who departed this city yesterday and the majority of those whom they placed in charge of the Republican Party and the Goldwater campaign. Before the convention, they seemed at a loss for a way to go after the racist vote in the North without making racism an article in the new Republican credo. But a way, it seems, has now been found, and the candidate who has moral scruples about the principle of segregation seems positively exhilarated by the thought of a campaign against mugging, stabbing, rape, housebreaking, and other well-known interracial activities. By this extraordinary means, he can seek the backlash vote without for one moment agreeing—or even, perhaps, acknowledging to himself—that that is what he is doing.

And he can do, one expects, even more than that. For the terrible problem he has brought into national politics creates anxiety everywhere. A white citizen may welcome the admission of Negroes into his trade union, may hope for the early accomplishment of integration in schools, may greatly admire the dignity and courage and intelligence of the leadership the Negro masses have been fortunate enough to find—he may do all these things and still tremble at the approach of a group of Negro youths on a lonely city street. The fear is not irrational; it has

something in common—indeed it has a great deal in common—
with the fear that a Negro citizen is bound to experience at the
approach of a group of white youths on a lonely country road
in Mississippi. Senator Goldwater, up to now a candidate of
little appeal in the Northern cities, will seek votes in them by
playing upon the fears of those condemned to live in them. He
offers himself as the man who, in the White House, may be able
to see to it that women "can go out in the streets . . . without
being scared stiff." It seems cruel to raise such a hope. As
President, he could do next to nothing toward its fulfillment.
The Constitution he reveres effectively blocks the way. He
might, to be sure, proclaim a broad federal responsibility for
seeking a solution to the multiple evils that have been visited
upon the cities in the course of their unplanned and uncon-
trolled growth. But here his view of the Constitution would
block the way. He believes that the cities and states should go
it alone in matters such as these. He opposed the present administration's request for the establishment of a Department of
Urban Affairs. He opposes federal aid to education and any
assumption of federal responsibility for poverty, unemployment,
or housing. He favors, he told *Der Spiegel,* "victory" in "struggle
between godless people and the people of God" (an aim of
the most dubious Constitutionality) and he favors "law and
order" on city streets. Law and order on the back roads of the
South is up to the sheriffs there.

Governor Rockefeller has said that he found the candidate's
acceptance speech "frightening." The word has been heard all
over the place every day. Most national conventions are frightening in one way or another. There is always at least one ruth-
less and tightly organized faction seeking to dominate by what
politicians nowadays call "muscle." No one seems above using
it—or above buying delegates or threatening them with political
and financial reprisals, forging tickets for hired demonstrators,
bribing or bullying sergeants-at-arms. There are few rights or
liberties for participants except those they take for themselves;
there is no machinery for remedying injustices. It is doubtful

if any methods were used here that were not used by the Eisenhower people in 1952 and the Kennedy people in 1960. The Goldwater people won by playing the game according to the rules, and the Scranton people lost not because they didn't use muscle, but because they simply didn't have enough of it to use. What has been really frightening here has not been the tactics but the tacticians. They are a new breed. It has been said—quite proudly—by the Goldwater people that this was the first convention for more than half of them; if the Northeastern states, which remained under the leadership of those who dominated the party in the period that is now part of the past, were excluded, the percentage of new talent would be much higher. Some of the new talent is quite old in years, but there was youth on every hand, and one suspects that many Goldwater delegates will be casting their first Presidential ballots in November. "Kooks" were rarely in evidence on the convention floor; roaming over it, one sometimes wished to come upon some recognizable human frailty, and when such a desire struck it was necessary to seek out some of the familiar and often rather frowzy aldermanic and county-commissioner types from the East and the Middle West. The rest were, for the very most part, smartly dressed, well adjusted, well organized, and well spoken. And they were hard as nails. The spirit of compromise and accommodation was wholly alien to them. They did not come to San Francisco merely to nominate their man and then rally his former opponents behind them. They came for a total ideological victory and the total destruction of their critics.

This was the real significance of the fight in the Resolutions Committee and of the floor fight over amendments to the platform. Some observers have said that they could not have afforded any show of division in their ranks, for this might have led to the kind of defeat the late Senator Taft met twelve years ago when the Eisenhower people managed to introduce a "moral issue" over the credentials of rival delegations from Texas. There is a tendency for defection to become contagious, and it has been argued that it was the fear of contagion rather

than of some slippage from pure Goldwaterism that made the
Goldwater people adamant about the platform. This may be so,
but the chances are that they would not have yielded anything
even if the platform had been adopted after the nomination.
They wished to punish as well as to prevail. The civil-rights
amendment proposed by Governor Romney could in no way
have offended or embarrassed Goldwater. It was a states'-rights
amendment wholly in keeping with the platform as it had come
from committee and with views the candidate himself has expressed a hundred times. But it came from Romney and was
supported by Rockefeller and Lodge and Scranton; this was
quite enough to make it unacceptable. They were not in the
least impressed by being told that acceptance of any of the
amendments offered on the floor would advance party unity and
make it easier for Republicans in the industrial states to win
votes. They were determined to give no offense to members of
the John Birch Society, and they plainly regarded as very slight
the cost of antagonizing General Eisenhower, Governors Scranton and Rockefeller, Senators Hugh Scott and Kenneth Keating,
or Representatives John Lindsay and Ogden R. Reid, of New
York. John Rousselot, the Birch lobbyist at the convention, said
that one hundred delegates belong to the Society. He may be
claiming too much or too little. But no matter—what the majority of delegates wanted was to assure Birchers that their participation in Republican affairs was welcome. Senator Peter H.
Dominick, of Colorado, assured a television audience that the
only Bircher he knew well was "a nifty guy." Most charac-
terizations of Nelson Rockefeller are unprintable.

There is considerable uncertainty at the moment as to what
it is that Goldwater and his men expect and want. If they share
the common assumptions about the American political process
and about the make-up of the American electorate, it would
seem that they have already conceded their defeat in November
and are heading toward some other, more distant goal. The men
they have scorned and insulted here are the very ones who
produced the only Republican victories since 1928. Probably

only a handful of them will find it advisable to quit the party or decline to give open support to the ticket. But far more than a handful will do as little as they can possibly get away with, and of these not a few will hope for the election of President Johnson. The Goldwater crowd knows all this, but it has persisted, even after getting everything it wanted from the convention, in deliberate and systematic alienation of support. The choice of William E. Miller as the Vice-Presidential candidate and of Dean Burch as party chairman seemed to many experienced politicians here to be evidence that defeat in the general elections was considered a certainty. Miller is an industrious, tough-talking, deserving party worker, but he has no following and hardly even an identity of his own. It would be surprising if he could carry even his own district on the ticket, for in his last election he won by only five thousand votes, as against a twenty-thousand majority the time before. Candidates for Vice-President rarely add to or detract very much from the vote of a Presidential candidate, but in tight elections, such as that of 1960, they can be important. There was no Lyndon Johnson for Goldwater to call upon this year, but he could have done better than Miller and this without appeasing his Eastern rivals. Senator Thruston B. Morton, of Kentucky, is a suitably conservative public servant who is known throughout the country and who conveys an impression of authority and solidity. He has, moreover, had some experience with foreign affairs. Miller has had none. The hard-core Goldwaterites may regard it as a stroke of good fortune to have Representative Miller serving the cause, and they no doubt feel that if their leader ever fell as John F. Kennedy did, Miller would be just the man to tell Castro where to head in and to pursue a "win" policy throughout the world. But there are Republican voters who will not easily be convinced of this. Miller was Goldwater's choice,* as

---

* Goldwater said that one of his reasons for choosing Miller was that "he drives Johnson nuts." Evidence of this was lacking, though there is no doubt that Miller had a peculiar effect on a good many other people. Aggressiveness was his long suit. "He's a tiger on the attack in an attack-

was Dean Burch. From all accounts, Burch, a Tucson lawyer, has gifts for political organization. After what has happened here, there is no reason to question the accounts. But there are many other good organizers in the Republican Party, and if the aim is to broaden the base of support, it is hard to think of one who could not have contributed more than Burch.

One Eastern Republican with an imposing record for keeping himself in office refused, all day Thursday, to believe that Goldwater really wanted Miller on the ticket. He had acquired considerable respect for the Goldwater organization as well as a number of bruises and lacerations, and he did not think that people who had shown so much cunning would, on the morning after their party victory, be foolish enough to damage their prospects for victory in November by inviting Miller to stand for Vice-President. He advised his friends to place no bets until Miller's name was before the convention and the nominations were closed. He thought he knew what was afoot. Goldwater,

---

ing year," a leading Republican explained, according to James A. Perry's *Barry Goldwater*. To help make this record complete, Miller's full name is William Edward Miller. He served six terms in the House of Representatives and one term of three years as chairman of the Republican National Committee. He was not quite the unanimous choice of the convention. Three delegates from Tennessee declined to vote for him. To quote again from Perry's report: "One disgusted Southerner said the Tennessee votes were cast against Mr. Miller because he is a Catholic. 'That's why they won't identify themselves,' he said. 'Poll the delegation individually back home, accuse them individually of voting for a Catholic, and you might come up with all twenty-eight saying they were among the three.' "

All of which brings back a memory. The night Goldwater was nominated, with five abstentions in the New York delegation, I went to the splendid Palace (now Sheraton-Palace) Hotel to meet a friend in the New York delegation, which maintained its headquarters there. I stood in the lobby as a leading New York politician, an immensely rich man, one whose family struck it very rich in oil, one who in fact coveted the prize Goldwater took that evening, a man whose monogram was the same as that of the incomparable painter Norman Rockwell, entered. A colleague asked this eminence, "Who were the abstainers?" And the reply came, "Oh, hell, five is just a number. Anyone can claim them who wants them."

91

he was sure, was simply playing for time. The ticket needed strength, but there were hurt feelings all over the place, and it would take some doing to get anyone of substance to agree to join it. It would have to be Miller or someone like him if no one else could be found; meanwhile, it was perfectly safe to announce that Miller was the favorite, because even one moment of such glory would satisfy Miller and because it would be no great blow to Miller's prestige if he were told in the end to withdraw. But the best information anyone has now is that Miller was the choice and the only choice by the time the convention opened and that the only man other than Burch considered as party chairman was Denison Kitchell, another Goldwater strategist. Burch was finally selected on the basis of politics within the small, tight Goldwater organization.

The Republican politician who misread Goldwater's intentions about Miller was willing, by the time the clerk was calling the roll on the Vice-Presidency, to entertain the possibility that Goldwater and his Western and Southern field commanders might know a few things about American politics that Easterners don't know. Until June 2, when Goldwater narrowly defeated Rockefeller in California, few of the Easterners thought that Goldwater had much chance of winning the Republican nomination. Had the established leaders thought otherwise, they would have behaved otherwise. As he left the St. Francis Hotel yesterday, General Eisenhower conceded that the declaration of "neutrality" he made more than a year ago had been a strategic error. Had he thought his declaration would work in Goldwater's favor, he would never have made it. Had Ambassador Lodge not thought that someone was bound to eliminate Goldwater, he would have left South Vietnam long before he did. Had Lodge or Scranton or Nixon filed for the California primary, one of them would almost certainly be the candidate today. But most of them assumed that he would be eliminated somewhere along the line, and it was this mistaken assumption that made possible his victory. It was also believed by many that to get the nomination, or to get even close to it, Goldwater would have to move from the far right to the center, or to a point very close to the center. If he was serious in his ambitions, he would have to become a "moderate." Goldwater seems to have known better. He has the nomination, and the only noticeable change in him is a stiffening of his position. He made his first outright defense of "extremism" and his first outright attack on "moderation" in his acceptance speech. In the aftermath of victory, most politicians seek to restore or to create unity, and acceptance speeches generally provide the first opportunity to make this effort. In victory, Goldwater's first act was to declare another war.

Those who have opposed him for the nomination believe that his chances of winning the election are slight and getting slighter by the day. They think he is throwing away votes every time he opens his mouth. But this analysis rests on a view of political realities that has been shown, by the fact of Goldwater's success, to be at least in part of questionable soundness. It assumes the existence of some sort of American "consensus"—a loose but prevalent ideology that may be described as the sum of the convictions that are commonly held by, for example, Senator Dirksen on the right and Senator Humphrey on the left. It further assumes that both major parties are organizations that exist to develop, express, and from time to time revise and amend the consensus. Goldwater has subscribed to no important part of this body of doctrine. He has used his Senate vote and his voice on Republican rostrums everywhere to oppose it from start to finish. Now he is master of his party. It may be that he is the rule-proving exception. But it may also be that the consensus is a fiction—that it is nothing but a conclusion drawn from a reading of recent history by historians eager to impose order upon experience. Or it may be that the consensus is a reality but that it is only one of many important realities, only one of many conceivable consensuses. If this is the case, it is at least theoretically possible for Goldwater to put together a winning combination of an entirely new sort. He will have the brass-collar Republican vote. His domination of the party liberates him to try for all the racists and all the jingoes. No one knows their number, but it may be great. Outside the cities, he can play on the hatred of them in the small towns; inside the cities, he can play on the frustrations of the white-collar workers, on the fears of what remains of the urban middle classes, and on the anxieties and subterranean prejudices of the working classes. He is in an excellent position to argue that he, and not his rival, is the poor man's candidate. One of the most remarkable of recent developments is Lyndon Johnson's emergence as the candidate of Eastern business. He seems well thought of on Wall Street and has widespread press support. Goldwater, with his money from the Southwestern speculators and promoters, may be able to press an advantage that no Republican candidate has ever enjoyed—the hostility of the Eastern money-changers. There may be nothing like a majority to be rallied in this fashion. Most authorities believe that his approach assures his defeat. But the authorities are not quite so sure of themselves as they were a short while back.

Goldwater and his lieutenants seemed to delight in outraging most of the party leaders of the Eisenhower years. They seemed to want these men to leave the party and to take their followers with them. They showed some concern, though, about the General himself. It was not notable for its depth. Eisenhower spent last Thursday, the day following Goldwater's nomination, in his hotel room. The quiet there was never interrupted by any word or message from Goldwater headquarters. In the evening, Eisenhower stayed in his room and watched television—intermittently at least. He was doing something else, his friends said, while Goldwater was defending extremism and consequently was not aware of the passage until he came upon it in a newspaper text. Still and all, the Goldwater people attached some value to his support or to his benevolent neutrality, and when Goldwater heard that the former President was upset by the acceptance speech, he found time, the following day, to call on Eisenhower and explain that in the House of Extremism there are many mansions. "When you led those troops across the channel into Normandy," Goldwater is reported by Denison Kitchell to have said to Eisenhower, "you were being an extremist." "I had never thought of it that way," the General replied. It is unclear whether he meant that an illumination had just been provided or whether he meant that only a nut could think of it that way.

No one has spoken with assurance of what course Eisenhower will now pursue. This may reflect his own uncertainty. What is anything but uncertain is that he came to San Francisco full of good will. Goldwater had not been his beau ideal of a candidate, and he made it as clear as he ever makes anything that he would have preferred Scranton and thought that his nonintervention would work against Goldwater's nomination. By convention time, though, he had put regrets behind him and was ready to accept the will of the delegates. He seemed willing to take any Republican's word for anything. In a news conference held just before the convention was called to order, he declared his support of the platform. He hadn't actually read it all, but Representative Melvin R. Laird, its principal architect, had called upon him and told him about it. "The way he explained it to me," the beaming old soldier said, "it sounded all right." He had wanted assurance that it was based on sound morality, and he got it. Laird had explained, Eisenhower said, that "the moral tone was there." But subsequent developments—the shouting-down of Governor Romney's amendments, the defense of extremism, and perhaps the wounds to his vanity—compelled him to reconsider. Every few hours here, there has been a new report of his state of mind and spirit, and although the latest one has him behind Goldwater, no one believes that this is the end of the story. There may never be any end, but whether there is or not, its unfolding in the months ahead should tell a good deal about the United States in 1964. For this agreeable, charitable, perpetually smiling and perpetually perplexed man who is of indeterminate social class, who is a small-towner one moment and a spokesman for the Eastern "power structure" the next, who is a conservative-liberal and a liberal-conservative and sometimes a conservative-conservative, embodies just about every possible consensus that anyone can imagine. Herb Caen, a columnist for the San Francisco *Chronicle,* the other day described Goldwater as being "as American as apple strudel." No one ever would or ever could say this of Eisenhower. And if he takes to the hustings for Goldwater, Caen's *mot* may turn out not to be *juste.*

We are at war in Vietnam—yet the President who is the Commander-in-Chief of our forces refuses to say whether or not the objective is victory. His Secretary of Defense continues to mislead and misinform the American people.

—Goldwater, acceptance speech, July 16, 1964

Nowhere in the world today is there a clearer road to *peace through strength* than in Vietnam.

—Goldwater, *Where I Stand*, 1964

* GOLDWATER OVER TONKIN, OR A PROBABLE CONSEQUENCE OF SAN FRANCISCO

(The report that follows appears exactly as it was printed in the August 22, 1964 issue of the *New Yorker*. I continue to think it a basically sound description and appraisal of the events with which it deals.)

August 13, 1964

The President has signed the joint congressional resolution that encourages him to "take all necessary measures" to defend American forces and to "prevent further aggression" in Southeast Asia, and he has stated his determination to be governed by its language. "To any armed attack upon our forces, we shall reply," he said in the presence of the military and congressional leaders who were gathered round his desk at the signing. "To any in Southeast Asia who ask our help in defending their freedom, we shall give it." It is the fourth resolution of its peculiar kind to be passed since 1955. In that year, Congress resolved that President Eisenhower be "authorized [to] employ the armed forces of the United States as he deems necessary for the specific purpose of securing and protecting Formosa and the Pescadores against armed attack." Two years later, he was authorized to "use armed forces to assist any nation [or] group of nations requesting assistance against armed aggression from any country controlled by international communism [in] the Middle East." In 1962, the House and Senate declared that "the United States is determined [to] prevent by whatever means may be necessary, including the use of arms, the Marxist-Leninist regime in Cuba from extending, by force or the threat of force, its aggressive or subversive activities in any part of the hemisphere." Now Southeast Asia—"our first line of defense," according to Senator Frank J. Lausche, of Ohio, an enthusiastic supporter of the resolution, who added that "when an enemy attacks us there, he is, in principle, attacking us on our native land"—has been favored with a resolution of its own, and it may be that in time the entire non-Communist world, and perhaps the non-Communist moon, will have congressional and Presidential assurance of American protection.

In the debate over each of these resolutions, it has been pointed out by some people that Congress was giving the President an authority he already had as Commander-in-Chief, and by others that it was surrendering its own Constitutional authority to declare war. On the one hand, no President needs the approval of Congress to repel attacks on American forces. And if he judges it necessary to assist other nations in order to maintain our own security, he is free to do so; all he need request from Congress is the money with which to render assistance. On the other hand, the resolutions can be read as advance authorizations of American belligerency in wars that have not yet begun—indeed, as in the case of the Cuban resolution, in situations where there is nothing more than an anticipated "threat of force." Whatever the merits of these contentions, the resolutions have been efficacious in a number of ways. It is generally believed that the 1955 resolution on Formosa and the Pescadores was largely responsible for a lessening of tensions in the South China Sea. It was an ingeniously worded document, notifying the Communist Chinese that we would defend the Nationalist presence on Formosa, and, in conjunction with the Mutual Defense Treaty negotiated with the Nationalists two months earlier, advising Chiang Kai-shek that we had no intention of supporting him in any effort to re-establish himself on the mainland and would not join in the defense of every rock in the Strait of Formosa that he chose to garrison. The adoption of the resolution on the Middle East—or the Eisenhower Doctrine, as it was called at the time—was followed by a period of relative ease and some uneasy accommodations in that part of the world; most people feel that its adoption had something to do with the improvement in the atmosphere there. It would be hard to claim that the Cuban resolution had any favorable impact on events, but if it did no ascertainable good, it surely did no harm.

What makes these resolutions particularly attractive to Presidents, though, is their effect on domestic politics. Their passage, which is always close to being unanimous, puts partisan critics at a disadvantage and enables the President to maintain that he is acting not only under his Constitutional powers and responsibilities but as a faithful executor of the declared will of Congress. In 1950, President Truman ordered American forces into action in Korea and then informed Congress of what he had done and what he planned to do. Within a matter of months, the Korean hostilities were being called "Truman's war" and the President found himself accused of a usurpation of congressional authority. Presidents Eisenhower, Kennedy, and Johnson profited by this lesson, and it is likely that their successors, whenever they discern any possibility of the engagement of American forces in combat of any kind, will request predated congressional approval.

The Southeast Asia resolution, the President said, shows "where America stands," and he went on to say that "the unanimity of the Congress reflects the unanimity of the country." The vote in Congress was indeed just about unanimous. In the Senate, only a pair of chronic dissenters—Wayne Morse, of Oregon, and Ernest Gruening, of Alaska—withheld approval. In the House, all those present voted for the resolution with the exception of another troublesome character—Adam Clayton Powell, who answered the roll with "Present." But the support the President got was by no means an expression of confidence in the administration's past, present, or future policies in Southeast Asia. All that was really being approved was the President's orders, which had already been given and carried out, for the Seventh Fleet to meet fire with fire. Apart from that, there is hardly even a majority position—to say nothing of "unanimity"—in the country, in Congress, or, for that matter, in the administration itself. In Congress—and presumably in the country—there is a sizable bloc of opinion that supports Senator Goldwater's demands for a "win" strategy and would commit American forces to war in North Vietnam. There is another bloc—fairly well represented in Congress and with at least a few adherents in the administration—that favors an early American withdrawal from South Vietnam, accompanied, perhaps, by an appeal to the United Nations to see what, if anything, it can do to assist the government of that country to hold on to some part of its sovereignty. Most of the members of this bloc gave the President the support he wanted, but did so with a singular lack of conviction. "I do not wish my vote for the resolution to be interpreted as an endorsement of our long-standing and apparently growing military involvement in Vietnam," Senator George McGovern, of South Dakota, said. "I have had serious misgivings about our entanglement in Vietnam since we were first committed to that course ten years ago." Senator McGovern, having noted that "any settlement in Southeast Asia that ignores China is largely useless," proposed "a safeguarded agreement with the Chinese on Southeast Asia." And there is a third view, which may have a few more adherents than either of the others. This holds that although we can never achieve the kind of "victory" that Goldwater calls for, we cannot afford the kind of defeat we would sustain if we pulled out now, when the politicians we support in what is essentially a civil war control only about 30 per cent of South Vietnamese territory by day and still less by night. In this view, we are thus compelled to assist the government of General Nguyen Khanh, or of any anti-Communist who succeeds him by whatever means, and hope for a day when it will be able to make a somewhat better claim than it can now make of being the effective government. If and when such a day comes, according to this school of opinion, the United States should urge Saigon to enter into immediate negotiations with its neighbors —through the United Nations or some specially convened group of interested powers.

There is every reason to believe that this last view is substantially the one held by the President. It is known to be the one held by such close associates of his as Senators J. William Fulbright and Humphrey, both of whom, in the Senate debate, expressed misgivings not unlike those of Senator McGovern. It was the view of John F. Kennedy. It is the view of ex-Ambassador Lodge and of Ambassador Maxwell Taylor. It is the view that prevails in the Defense and State Departments, where it would be hard to find anyone who favors extending the war or who defines "victory" as anything more grandiose than a return to the *status quo ante*. Addressing the American Bar Association yesterday, the President dissociated himself both from those who, like General Khanh and Senator Goldwater, would carry the war north and from those who, like Senator Morse, would withdraw from it tomorrow. His stress was on the unwisdom of extending it, and his hope, therefore, must be for eventual negotiation. Yet the fact is that within the past two weeks the President has himself extended the war by ordering American attacks on installations in North Vietnam. (The White House would no doubt point out that it was actually the North Vietnamese who extended the war by assaulting American ships in international waters. This was the case, but the President's "measured response" was made partly at sea and partly on mainland bases, and it was this last that the Secretary of State was referring to when he spoke of the "sting" that the Hanoi regime had felt.) The President, moreover, sought and was given congressional approval for further extensions of the war and for further military involvement in Southeast Asia.

No diplomatic interest of this government or of the Johnson administration was served by the part of the resolution that American forces will fire when fired upon. There cannot be a capital anywhere that supposes the United States would put ships to sea, planes in the air, or troops in the field merely to serve as targets. As for the rest of the resolution, it is diplomatically irrelevant and, in the main, meaningless. It cites previously negotiated treaties that commit us to assist other signatory powers "in defense of freedom," and it assures the President that Congress will stand behind him in combating "further aggression." Just about everyone here and abroad knows, though, that the problem in South Vietnam is civil war and armed subversion, not "aggression." If an end could be put to that country's agony simply by clearing it of foreign armies, Senator Goldwater's strategy would make good sense and the President's very little. But if there seems to be a contradiction between the President's appraisal of the actual situation and his recent actions—the orders to strike at North Vietnamese bases and the request for congressional approval—it is a contradiction that no one here has much difficulty in explaining. At least part of the explanation is to be found in the person of Senator Goldwater, who said yesterday that things were looking up because the President had been "following my advice." No bulletins from Saigon confirmed Goldwater's sanguine view, but there was word from the Louis Harris organization that must have been extremely gratifying to the White House. A poll it conducted in the few days after the President's "measured response" revealed a striking growth of public confidence in his conduct of affairs in Southeast Asia. An earlier poll had seemed to show that Goldwater and other critics had been quite successful in undermining confidence. Before the exchange in the Gulf of Tonkin, according to Harris, only 42 per cent of the public approved of Johnson's stewardship. Immediately after the exchange, the figure went up to 72. Goldwater had been talking about South Vietnam as the central foreign-policy issue of the campaign. It had never sounded like a very promising one, for although a good many citizens seem to have opinions on what ought to be done, there is no evidence that feeling on the matter runs high enough to switch votes. Even so, it looked good to Goldwater, and perhaps it still does. It is too early to say that the President has taken it away from him, but it does seem reasonably clear that if the President had done less than he did the Harris organization would have had a different story to tell, and so would Goldwater.

The PT boats that pursued the destroyer *Maddox* on August 2 and those that attacked the *Maddox* and the *C. Turner Joy* two days later were units of the North Vietnamese Navy, and no one here has suggested that their commanders were under orders to create an occasion for the President to improve his standing with American voters. Nor has it been suggested that the President would have ignored the occasion if it had taken place the day after his election. There are, however, some serious questions about the sequence of events in the Gulf of Tonkin two weeks ago, and about the interpretation of those events here. Throughout the period in which the resolution was before Congress, the government insisted that North Vietnam was waging naval warfare against the United States. It had an unlikely sound—one of the world's weakest sea powers engaging the world's strongest—but no one except Senator Morse, who spoke in the Senate each day and kept describing the American role as that of a "provocateur" in Southeast Asia, disputed it. Last Friday, though, as the House and the Senate were voting on the resolution, Defense Department officials informed the press that, in the words of a Washington *Post* story, "what the United States branded and still regards as a 'deliberate' attempt to challenge the nation on the high seas may not have been regarded in that light by those who ordered the attacks." It was explained that on the day before the first pursuit of the *Maddox,* armed junks and torpedo boats of the South Vietnamese Navy had raided the North Vietnamese islands of Hon Me and Hon Ngu. Shortly after the raids, the *Maddox* had patrolled waters close to those islands. Its commander, the Pentagon said, had not been advised of the raids (though American military advisers in Saigon knew they were taking place), but the North Vietnamese were not privy to communications between Washington and Saigon, and the presence of the *Maddox* close to the islands under siege might very well have been taken as conclusive evidence that the United States had already decided to extend the war to North Vietnam and was providing naval cover for the attack.

In the period immediately following the first attack on the *Maddox,* the White House and the Pentagon acknowledged that the North Vietnamese might have made a mistake of some kind, though no one then mentioned the South Vietnamese naval raids. The second attack, however, was described as certain proof that the first had not been a mistake and that the Hanoi government was committing unprovoked aggression. No one here last week had any knowledge on which to base a doubt of this contention. (Senator Morse's talk of American guilt was based on his belief that the whole American presence on the Indochinese peninsula is illegal and constitutes a standing provocation.) Doubts persisted, nevertheless, and last Friday, as both houses of Congress were casting their votes on the resolution, Pentagon officials confirmed the fact that the South Vietnam raids had taken place, and explained that while the *Maddox* had played no part in them, the mission that had brought it close to the raiding parties was, as one correspondent who attended the briefing wrote, "to see if the new talk in North and South Vietnam about expanding the war had resulted in increased Communist operations." The *Maddox* radar, the Pentagon explained, had spotted North Vietnamese ships clearing the waters off Hon Me after one of the raids, and it was acknowledged that the commanders of those vessels might have reasonably assumed that the *Maddox* had been used either to shell the island or to escort the attacking vessels. The Pentagon maintained, though, that no such misunderstanding could account for the second attack. The United States had by then explained the nonbelligerent status of the Seventh Fleet, and the *Maddox* and the *C. Turner Joy* were more than sixty miles offshore. But this interpretation involves the assumption that the North Vietnamese authorities not only got our message but accepted it at face value and were still determined to extend the war to the United States. And it leaves unexplained—except, possibly, to those who place more faith than experience seems to justify in the deterrent effect of congressional resolutions, which have never yet stopped a war in progress—the fact that there have been no further attacks. Under questioning, Pentagon officials acknowledged that there was at least a possibility that the second attack had been a "face-saving" gesture, rather than part of a systematic plan to destroy American sea power. This did not satisfy the military correspondent for the Washington *Star,* who wrote, in the issue announcing the passage of the resolution, that "the whole Tonkin Gulf incident which precipitated the crisis in Southeast Asia might never have occurred except for confusion—on both the American and Communist sides—over a little-noted incident last Saturday."

The crisis was a brief one, and it seems unlikely that historians will assign it a place of much importance. It has had no effect on the balance of power in Southeast Asia, and there appears to be little chance that it will cause the President to order further changes in the conduct of American policy in South Vietnam. But it led to the first direct confrontation of American and Communist military units since Korea; indeed, because our troops in Korea fought under a United Nations command, it might even be described as the first such confrontation in history. It probably would not have occurred except for the "little-noted incident" in the waters off North Vietnam. And it probably would not have occurred except for a much-noted incident in the United States—the nomination of Senator Goldwater in San Francisco last month. For the fact is that this government, though it exercised restraint in retaliation and was at pains to make clear that restraint was part of its policy, declared the existence of a major crisis before it knew that one existed. The reaction of its leaders was uncharacteristic of them; their deliberations were strikingly brief in comparison with those at the time of the missile crisis in 1962, for example —and, according to the participants, there was no questioning of the strategy that was employed. The circumstances were, to be sure, quite different from those of 1962. The probable consequences of mistakes and misunderstandings were almost certainly less grave, and the options were less numerous and, for that reason, easier to choose among. This, however, could have allowed for more, rather than less, investigation and deliberation. The cost of delay in military terms could not have been high; indeed, our only losses came as a result of the mainland bombings, and this was an aspect of our strategy that might have been the subject of further deliberation. But, with Senator Goldwater heading the Republican ticket and mobilizing war hawks wherever he goes, the cost in political terms might very well have been not only high but, by White House estimates, prohibitive.

What the liberals had better understand is that we're here to stay, that we're a serious force in American political life, with respectable politicians and intellectual organs at our command.

> —William Rusher, publisher of the *National Review*, quoted in *Partisan Review*, Fall, 1964

These people who constitute the extreme right are good people. They are generally fairly well-to-do people. They are very sincere in their beliefs.

> —Goldwater, quoted in *Mr. Conservative*, a biography by Jack Bell

August 20, 1964

Stephen C. Shadegg, a sometime Hollywood writer, actor, press agent, "lie detector expert" (he so described himself in a recent interview), and manufacturer of an asthma remedy named Adreno-Mist, is a figure of importance in the Republican Party today. He directed Barry Goldwater's campaigns for the United States Senate in 1952 and 1958 and served a term as Republican state chairman in Arizona. In 1960 and 1962, his services were retained by several other candidates, mainly of the Goldwater persuasion, and this year he directed Goldwater's campaign for the nomination in the Western states. He has been busy writing, too. He is the author of an authorized biography of Goldwater, and for a number of years he turned out a regular newspaper column signed by Goldwater and headed "How Do You Stand, Sir?" He has written a great many Goldwater speeches, magazine articles, and press releases, and also portions of Goldwater's essay on diplomacy, *Why Not Victory?* Now he has favored us with a treatise on strategy, *How to Win an Election: The Art of Political Victory*. It does not dissolve all the mysteries (in 1962 Shadegg sought a nomination for himself and couldn't get it), but it does yield certain insights on the Goldwater movement, which, for an unhappy season at least, is Republicanism. In it, for example, Shadegg acknowledges a heavy obligation to an older and better-known craftsman, Mao Tse-tung. He has profited greatly, so he tells us, from a close study of Mao on "the tactics of infiltration." "In the Goldwater campaign," he writes, "and in all other campaigns where I have served as a consultant, I have followed the advice of Mao Tse-tung."

It is not, really, a very likely story. Mao is a man of formidable cunning and intellect, but he does not have much in the way of a message for American politicians hustling money from frightened small-town bankers and merchants, writing hard-sell copy for television, and mobilizing housewives for duty at headquarters' switchboards and mimeograph machines. It seems to please Shadegg, though, to identify himself with a noted revolutionary thinker, and in this he resembles a number of other American rightists. "I would suggest," Goldwater himself has said, "that we analyze and copy the strategy of the enemy; theirs has worked and ours has not." The John Birch Society boasts of its borrowings, in organizational structure and technique, from the Communist Party, and in tone, in rhetoric, and even in format, its official publication, *American Opinion,* puts one in mind of nothing so much as the Communist theoretical organ *Political Affairs.* A Goldwater militant named Donald Lukens, head of the Young Republicans, has recommended a "ten-year plan" to train "conservative" writers to "take over" the American press, which men of Lukens's sort now look upon as a citadel of corrupt liberalism. A few years back, no one in Republican or Democratic politics would have spoken of "infiltration" as a defensible method. The method was, of course, employed, but the word was a dirty one, drawn from an alien lexicon; it would never have fallen from the lips of such American masters of organization as Marcus Alonzo Hanna or James Aloysius Farley. Things are different now. Shadegg advises, as an early step in any campaign run on Maoist principles, the formation of a "cell group." But then it turns out that most of the cell groups he set up for Goldwater were similar to the traditional, "non-partisan" citizens' committees—"enthusiastic, knowledgeable Goldwater supporters who would not be labeled or identified as members of any special organization." Some "cell" members spied on the opposition, rifled its wastebaskets for intelligence purposes, and used their positions in the community to advance the cause. (*E.g.*, a rightist barber accompanied the music of the shears with discourses on the worthlessness of foreign aid.) Old goods, new labels.

Shadegg could not have learned much from Chairman Mao, but the name is an okay one to drop, and Bolshevik language is stylish in Goldwater circles. In part, this is because ex-Communists have had a large part in building the movement and in giving it whatever it can be said to have in the way of ideology. (The weekly *National Review* has led the way in this; the leading ideologues on that journal have been James Burnham, Frank S. Meyer, and the late Whittaker Chambers—all ex-Communists. Its correspondent at the convention that nominated Goldwater was John Dos Passos.) In part, too, it is because paranoia is epidemic on the far right; these people believe that the Marxists *are* winning everywhere—and winning because of their political wizardry. But there is more to it than that. The language of sedition is relevant—not to Shadegg's managerial problems in local campaigns, but to what has happened in and to the Republican Party over the last three or four years. It has indeed been "infiltrated . . . captured," and made (as Richard Hofstadter says) a "front organization" by an organized faction whose loyalty to Goldwater and Goldwaterism far transcends its loyalty to Republicanism. The methods were essentially those of the Communist factions which in the thirties and forties gained control of minor parties, major trade unions, and other organizations.

The primary resources of the seditionists were zeal and energy. One of the prices we Americans pay for our unideological parties is a shortage of these two qualities, particularly the latter. Generally speaking, anyone who is willing to give a few hours a month to party work will be rewarded with some measure of authority. "Let George do it" is the motto of the "moderates," and if George does it—if he attends all the meetings, puts stamps on envelopes, and uncomplainingly empties the ashtrays—he will soon enough find himself drafting the resolutions, chairing the meetings, and being given his choice of committee assignments. The Goldwater people were the sort to arrive early at meetings, endure all the tedium, and stay on, bright-eyed, after adjournment, to fold the chairs and put the coffee cups away. Great stores of subversive power are to be found in these useful traits. In time, the chair-folders are writing platforms, conducting purges, and threatening to wreck the organization if their rule is challenged.

San Francisco was not really the site of the rightists' seizure of power; it was the city in which it was demonstrated that the event had already taken place. The Goldwater "Georges" had become delegates to the national convention, and they were in the majority. How great and how solid their majority there was it is at present difficult to say. There is some dispute as to when inevitability set in. Within the clear Goldwater majority, there were degrees of militance. There were some who would joyfully lose with Goldwater, who would far sooner establish the principle that "extremists" were welcome than deny the principle in the hope that the denial would produce the margin of victory. By and large, these were the people who had taken over the party in states where Republicans never won anything (the deep South) and in states where they generally win everything (the mountain states of the West). But there were also those from states (notably in the Middle West) where elections are hard fought and where power is worth having, and although these delegates were mainly Goldwaterites, they were not entirely beyond appeals to reason, prudence, and the lust for success. It was they whom Governor Scranton tried to pull out of the Goldwater majority in the few weeks before the convention. Since he had only Governor Rockefeller and Henry Cabot Lodge as allies in that stage, there was no hope for him. But an earlier start might have changed things greatly—as might some clear thinking on General Eisenhower's part and some unselfish thinking on Richard Nixon's. And if Nelson Rockefeller had done just one-half per cent better in the California primary on June 3, there would probably be no Goldwater today. This might just possibly have come to pass if a Rockefeller baby had not been born on the eve of that election.

The radical right needed luck, quite a lot of it, to prevail. For despite their zeal and energy, and despite their willingness to learn from the Marxist-Leninist-Maoist classics, these people have always been appallingly incompetent politicians. They are faction-ridden themselves, and they have never, up to now, had strong or central leadership. This is the first time they have ever won anything of value, and it remains to be seen whether what they have won is really worth having, even in the short run. We can be reasonably sure, it seems to me, that in the long run, provided there is one, Goldwaterism is bound to fail. It cannot solve any of the major problems of this country—if for no other reason (though there are plenty of other reasons) than that it denies their existence. Goldwater's election in November is conceivable; if, however, democratic institutions survived the event (and one assumes that they would, unless he and Khrushchev contrived to vaporize us all) his re-election would be altogether inconceivable. He might, of course, elect to junk all his "conservative" twaddle and become a Republican Lyndon Johnson. Stranger things have happened. But then he would no longer be Goldwater; he would be the slayer of Goldwaterism.

Still and all, it is no mean feat to take over the Republican Party, and the Goldwater Maoists—abetted by luck and by extraordinary mismanagement on the part of the opposition— pulled it off. They have central leadership for the first time, and within the party they have captured they may be able to achieve a unity that up to now has eluded them.

The relationship of Goldwater to Goldwaterism is something of a mystery. He is anything but the Lenin of the rightist Bolsheviki. He is not a theorist, not an organizer, not even, really, much of a leader. He has a fairly quick mind but an indolent and ill-disciplined one. He has always been pleased to have others do his thinking for him. This is why he seems end-lessly—and to his own endless surprise—caught up in contradictions. He has let just about anyone who described himself as a "conservative" issue statements in his name, contribute to his books and articles, and compose speeches for him. He is himself no fanatic; his natural approach is casual, self-effacing, speculative. He is capable of making a long series of fiercely doctrinaire pronouncements and then describing them as nothing more than a few random thoughts he felt might be worth consideration—or "kicking around," as he likes to say. He has never seemed to hunger for power in the way that men like the Kennedys and Lyndon Johnson do. Such men are rarely hobbyists; Goldwater is a dedicated one and often seems to resent politics for the way it intrudes on the time he wishes to give to his short-wave broadcasting, skin-diving, flying, photography, and automobile tinkering. I was alone with him once, about three years ago, for about an hour and a half, and I was unable to drag a political opinion from him. Some erroneous instructions had brought us to a television studio far too early, and we had no choice but to pass the time in conversation. I welcomed the opportunity, but was unable to make good use of it. He was interested in knowing what make of car I had, whether I found it satisfactory, whether it had this attachment or that, and so on. With that subject exhausted, we went on to sports and several other matters. I could not induce him to talk politics. It was not that he was being cagey or avoiding journalistic traps—he is the least cagey of politicians, and hardly a day passes when he does not walk upright into a trap. I took him, and still take him, to be a man easily bored. I suspect he entered politics in the first place to escape his boredom with his hobbies and with merchandising, and that after a time boredom with politics of the ordinary sort led him, on the one hand, to the politics of the bizarre and, on the other, back to the hobbies.

I do not mean to suggest that his "conservatism" is any kind of pose or affectation. Up to a point at least, it seems a natural enough product of his temperament, his education (and lack of it), and his environment. But his association with the *far* right —with anti-Semites, white supremacists, witch hunters, fundamentalist preachers, jingoes, and even food faddists—is a puz-

"THEY'RE NOT IN THE BUSINESS OF OVERTHROWING THE GOVERNMENT, AND WE'RE NOT IN THE BUSINESS OF DISCOURAGING VOTES."

zling business. It is an association of relatively recent origin. He entered the Senate in 1952 as an Eisenhower Republican—hot for "fiscal responsibility" but hot, too, for "peace," for some measure of social justice (bank-deposit insurance, workmen's compensation, etc.), and racial amity (member of and contributor to the National Association for the Advancement of Colored People, the National Urban League, etc., etc.). He was not a firebrand of any sort—but then, sometime close to the end of the decade, he became one, and of a very peculiar sort. The transformation was engineered, it seems reasonably clear, by the young rightist intellectuals (and the older ex-Communist ones) associated with William F. Buckley, Jr.'s *National Review*. Goldwater was a restless politician without any ideas distinct enough to give him an identity; the *National Review* crowd had plenty of political ideas (I use the word loosely; their conservatism, as Karl Meyer has said, "is a mood, not an ideology") but no politicians to give them currency. They began writing Goldwater's books and speeches and in the process committed him more and more deeply to their particular brand of rightist dissent and negation. The doctrines they saddled Goldwater with differed in certain ways from those of the unwashed, untutored racists who now stomp and shout at Goldwater rallies and from those of the oil and cattle barons who put up the money for it all. The Buckley group doesn't recommend racial segregation as a way of life (though it tends to be rather soft on South Africa), and James Burnham's enthusiasm for *jihad* is not necessarily shared by the comfortable Texas and California promoters who would like their comfort increased by abolition of the graduated income tax. But the necessary accommodations have been made, and for the time being it is pointless to worry the question of whether Goldwater "believes" wholeheartedly or hardly at all in all the things he has been saying and that they have been saying for him. The point is that he became "hooked" and that he seems, now, to enjoy it.

It has been suggested that his relationship to the far right is very similar to the relationship, a decade and a half ago, of

Henry Wallace, Roosevelt's second Vice-President, to the far left. Wallace, who had once been a Republican, was not a Communist, but he didn't mind sounding like one, and he was pleased to let them organize a Presidential campaign for him. They did not recognize him as a leader, but they were delighted to have him as a front man. There is perhaps a bit more enthusiasm for Goldwater among the rightist malcontents than there was for Wallace among the leftists, but my impression is that the only way Goldwater can "lead" them is by echoing them. He did not take over the Republican Party; they did—and while they could not possibly have done so without him as their candidate, their loyalty is not to him but to the myths they live by. It is possible that a day will come when he will find that he himself, as a Presidential candidate or as a President, cannot live by their myths. If that should happen, they would call him Judas—pointing out, no doubt, the racial nexus.

As I write, on the eve of the Democratic convention, the omens are for a massive repudiation of Goldwater and Goldwaterism. The opinion polls are giving President Johnson an almost two-to-one lead just about everywhere but in the South— in most parts of which Goldwater appears to have a clear but not overwhelming lead. The polls have erred in the past, but never spectacularly in terms of percentages. In recent American history, two-to-one leads are unheard of. Fifty-five per cent is a landslide. There is great fear among the Democrats that their association with the "Negro revolution"—or, more properly, "resistance"—will draw voters to Goldwater. The latest soundings confirm the fear, but at the same time they indicate that for every Democratic voter who defects to Goldwater, there will be two or three Republicans defecting to Johnson. There are reasons, nevertheless, for anxiety. The precedents all come from another epoch. For half a century, the kind of issues that Goldwater will exploit have been kept out of Presidential campaigns. The political process seemed to draw Presidential aspirants to the middle ground. Debate was over means, not ends. One of the big differences between Eisenhower and Stevenson in 1952 was that Eisenhower, at somebody's bright suggestion, said that he would go to Korea to see how the war might best be ended, while Stevenson either didn't think of making such a proposal or didn't think he should. Kennedy and Nixon in 1960 conducted campaigns that were largely statistical in content—disagreeing over the rate of economic growth, the ratings abroad of American "prestige," and the quantitative and qualitative adequacy of American arms. This campaign will be like none we have ever known. It will, it now seems, be a referendum on bigotry. It will provide opportunities to register fear, bravado, frustration, and conflicting views of the past. These opportunities, once their existence is recognized, may lead many people to behave quite differently on November 3 from the way they now think they will behave.

It will in any event be a disagreeable autumn. There is little reason to hope that there will be no further consequences of Goldwater comparable to the Gulf of Tonkin "crisis." And there will be an utterly and damagingly irrelevant review of history— whether it was right or wrong to recognize the Soviet Union in 1933, whether the growth of federal power that began over a century ago was a good thing or a bad thing, whether or not the government in an industrial society should assume any responsibility for easing the adjustments that industrialism requires. We will be asking all the wrong questions and getting nowhere in seeking answers to the right ones. For a time, many people thought all this would be therapeutic. It would offer a chance to destroy the myths, to give all the Know-Nothings the last thrashing they would ever need. In his first days in the White House, President Johnson was reported to relish the prospect of a Goldwater candidacy. A few months later, though, it was being reported that he dreaded it, even though he continued to feel that there was no other man whom he could so handily and so thoroughly defeat.

I think the latter view is the sounder one. The country and the Republican Party deserve better than what they got at San Francisco. But I think, too, that if Johnson wins with a good-sized popular vote—not necessarily two to one or anything like it, but perhaps six or seven to five—we will hear little more of Goldwater, Goldwaterism, or the far right. The Goldwater "Georges" will remain in control of the Republican organizations here and there, but they will be on the defensive, and Goldwater's opponents will be vindicated. Republican leadership will gradually pass back to those who have shown that they know the way to victory—men like Governor Scranton and Senator Kuchel. Both were defeated at San Francisco, but both have in recent years won solider victories than Goldwater has ever won. They are men of high intelligence and seriousness, and it should be within their power, once Goldwater is out of the way and General Eisenhower is once again living with his memories, to make the Republican Party a useful and powerful instrument rather than the dangerous one it has become under men who are ignorant, irresponsible, and, as in the case of their present leader, essentially frivolous.

Hello, Lyndon! Well, hello, Lyndon,
It's so nice to have you here where you belong.

—ad infinitum

The ego of the man is without bounds. He will want to be the best president
the United States has ever had. . . . Failure is intolerable, and that goes for
anyone close to him. . . . The appetite for triumph is like the ego, without limits.

—Marquis W. Childs, St. Louis *Post-Dispatch*

* BIG PUMPKIN ON THE BOARDWALK:
A LETTER FROM ATLANTIC CITY

August 28, 1964

On Monday and Tuesday, the President watched the Democratic convention on television and was, like thousands in the vast studio audience here, and like millions of other Americans, bored. On Wednesday, he did what no other set owner in the country could do: He burst into the studio, ordered most of the cast off the set, and improvised an entirely new show—based on an orginal idea by Lyndon Johnson, directed by Lyndon Johnson, starring Lyndon Johnson. Lyndon Johnson had, of course, written, directed, and produced the early scenes that he, as a viewer, had found so tedious. He had also fussed for months over the set design, the lighting, the general decor of the studio, and the seating arrangements for the live audience. It was not for lack of craftsmanship on his part that the show was less than gripping. Everyone agrees that he is a superb craftsman (some people deliver the compliment on the back of the left hand), and he knows all the uses of tension and conflict. He had, though, his own reasons for not wanting to exploit them in this particular production. He had hoped to get by on suspense alone. Would it turn out to be the nice gardener? The rich uncle? The obsequious butler? The malevolent son-in-law? The gentle family doctor? His problem, a familiar one since the dawn of dramaturgy, was that if he broke the suspense before the final scene, he would have an anticlimax on his hands. This was dramatically intolerable—and especially so since the plan was that the last scene was to be entirely his—but it was equally intolerable to keep numbing the viewers with interminable soliloquies, and it was expecting far too much of them to suppose that they, like the Democratic politicians standing in agitated clusters beside the boardwalk Pokerino parlors and frozen-custard stands, would endure all this merely to satisfy their curiosity as to whether it would, in the end, be Senator Humphrey or Senator Eugene McCarthy or Senator Mike Mansfield or perhaps some college president or soldier or corporation executive. To most of the delegates here, the wait for the President's decision was almost unbearable; to some, indeed, and particularly to those who thought that Senator Humphrey's claim on the Vice-Presidential nomination was very nearly as undeniable as Lyndon Johnson's on the Presidential nomination, the President's delay in announcing his choice seemed close to being inhuman. But the country as a whole, the President knew, could not share the convention's mood; not many people would put up with hours of stupefying television on the chance that Roger Mudd would break in with a hot tip on the Vice-Presidency.

And so the President, on Wednesday morning, rewrote the script. He created new elements of suspense by floating new rumors about the Vice-Presidency and about his own plans. He added new sound effects: the clatter of helicopters and the boom of jets drowned out "Hello, Lyndon" and "Happy Days Are Here Again"—pleasant, even stirring airs but a bit trying after two days. He merged the last scene with the penultimate one, the climax with the anticlimax, so that the last two days were one noisy, colorful, varied, and quite rousing act—short on tension, barren (after Wednesday afternoon) of suspense, but fast paced and full of action, an extravaganza with bits of business drawn from *Hellzapoppin* and the only other major American drama that has had Atlantic City for a setting, Thornton Wilder's *The Skin of Our Teeth*. He even managed to outwit the only people over whom he had, up to then, no control—the camera crews and the men in the "anchor booths," who had been trying to liven things up by drawing attention away from the scheduled proceedings and fixing it on sideshows (mostly of a character distasteful to the President) in and around Convention Hall. His very presence in the hall made this sort of thing an act of rudeness, even of lèse-majesté. The viewing audience, along with most of those in the hall, was kept largely unaware of, for example, the fact that throughout the entire final evening seven or eight Freedom Democrats from Mississippi stood in a circle with heads bowed, lips tight, and hands locked in the center in the spot from which most of the seats for Mississippi Democrats had been removed. (Around them was another circle—of men, all white and presumably convention officials of some sort, who had locked arms to prevent other Freedom Democrats or sympathizers from enlarging the inner circle.) Thus was television brought under control and made to show what the President thought it proper to show.

He did not necessarily relish every part of the production of the last two days. He could not have begrudged Robert Kennedy or the memory of John F. Kennedy the wild, sustained applause that broke out when the Attorney General appeared on the podium. He knew that it was inevitable, and he almost certainly felt that it was desirable; for although he yearns for total mastery of the Democratic Party and for a freedom of initiative as nearly complete as such freedom can ever be, he wants not only to defeat Barry Goldwater in November but to crush him, and in this endeavor he will get what help he can (and it will probably be immense) from running as John F. Kennedy's chosen heir and as the Attorney General's friend and patron. Even before the convention, he had arranged things so that the Kennedy demonstration could do him no conceivable harm and would, in fact, by being juxtaposed with an ovation for him, augment the strength of the Johnson-Humphrey ticket of 1964 with that of the Kennedy-Johnson ticket of 1960. Senator Humphrey, drawing on Ralph Waldo Emerson's division of mankind into the "party of hope" and the "party of memory," was willing to let Goldwater and Miller run on the memory ticket. The President, who wants everything, would like to be the candidate of both the Emersonian parties and can be counted upon to find places on his own ticket for Franklin D. Roosevelt, Harry S. Truman, John F. Kennedy, and, if he can manage it, Dwight D. Eisenhower. Nevertheless, the Kennedy demonstration must have had its galling aspects. Delegates and journalists sat up until this morning's early hours trying to decide whether it was essentially a gesture of affection and sympathy for Robert Kennedy, whose largest hopes had been dashed by the President, or whether it was a kind of memorial service for the late President. It was probably both—though if it was a tribute to a fallen leader as well as a salute to a living one, it often seemed, with all its noise and its strident, festive colors and its general gaiety, as macabre a ceremony of its kind as one could imagine. Whatever it was, one of its meanings for Lyndon Johnson was that his mastery of the party is not quite complete and probably never will be. The party continues to be afflicted with a mild case of polycentrism. The divisions—if one puts aside what appears to be the total disaffection of some Southern organizations—are not comparable in seriousness to those in the Republican Party this year, but there are, it seemed clear last night, Democratic centers of power outside the White House.

And these follow, in a rather curious way, the lines of division in the Republican Party. The Democratic "Eastern Establishment" resists the Johnson authority as the Republican "Eastern Establishment" resists that of Goldwater. Robert Kennedy is not the Kenneth Keating of the Democrats, and it seems unlikely that he will ever wish or feel compelled to play the game as Keating plans to, but the two New York senatorial candidates have, in their relationship to the national leaders of their party, some important things in common. Both are building independent organizations. Both are trying to keep old traditions and viewpoints alive and viable. Both are allied, in national politics, with young and powerful governors who came into power under the aegis of national leaders who have passed from the national scene. These governors (Republicans like Rockefeller and Scranton; Democrats like Endicott Peabody, of Massachusetts, and Edward T. Breathitt, of Kentucky) at present owe nothing or (in the case of the Democrats) almost nothing to Goldwater or Johnson and will make what use they can of this political solvency for as long as they feel it to their advantage. And the Eastern Democrats, like the Eastern Republicans, have some powerful allies in the Far West, most notably in California and Oregon. Pierre Salinger, fortunately for him, will not be running against Senator Kuchel, but the incumbent Democratic and Republican Senators from California have in common, vis-à-vis the candidates for President their parties have chosen, about what Kennedy and Keating have in common.

The difference between Goldwater's problem and Johnson's is the difference between open rebellion in the here and now and a mild threat of resistance at some time in the future—in today's perspective of time, a future that should seem distant and quite manageable to Johnson. Unlike Goldwater, Johnson has been busy all year doing what he can to make sure that the possible will not become the probable. He did not go so far as to attempt to patch things up by accepting Robert Kennedy as his candidate for the Vice-Presidency. That would never have worked anyway; it would merely have displayed the division at the highest level of government, where it would undoubtedly have widened. And it would almost inevitably have produced, at some point during this convention, a demonstration for Hubert Humphrey comparable to last night's Kennedy demonstration and politically far more divisive. Humphrey has at least as large and loyal a following as the Attorney General, and there would have been no ambiguity in the kind of display these admirers would have put on if their man had been passed over. But Johnson did not pass over Hubert Humphrey for a Democratic William Miller (he would have had to go far outside the ranks of the leading aspirants to find a really comparable figure), and he thus put the ticket beyond criticism by party regulars of almost every sort. It will be a long while before it will be possible to make any informed conjectures as to what he would have done about the Vice-Presidency if he could have ignored the "consensus" to which he almost unfailingly defers—and hurriedly, too, when the inevitable is about to come to pass. He would probably have preferred a man with a smaller following, a quieter voice, fewer ideological commitments, and a bit less energy. His doubts about Humphrey must have turned around mornings in the years ahead, when, if the electorate vindicates his confidence on November 3, he might pick up the paper to discover that the Vice-President of the United States had proposed an entirely new system for handling international disputes or some sweeping revisions in the structure of the national economy. And the doubts could have turned not alone on the possibility that Humphrey would actually do this sort of thing but on the likelihood that if Humphrey accepted the restraints of the office—as, of course, he would, so far as it would be humanly possible for him to do so— he would be a most unhappy man and thus troublesome in some other, presently unforeseeable, ways.

By selecting Humphrey and by accepting the Credentials Committee's stern settlements of the disputes over the Alabama and Mississippi delegations, the President deprived those who retain some power to resist him of any politically defensible reasons for using it. All his potential rivals must be allied belligerents in 1964. There will be no Democratic "unity" or "summit" meetings of the sort the Republicans held in Hershey, Pennsylvania, a few weeks ago, for "unity" has been achieved everywhere but in the deep South, where it could have been bought only at an altogether prohibitive price, and a Democratic "summit" is in continuous and almost plenary session in Lyndon Johnson's head. At the beginning of this week, it was by no means clear that things were going to turn out this way. His unwillingness to break the suspense over the Vice-Presidency was read by many as an expression of determination to name someone other than Humphrey. He seemed to want to go no further than the Republicans had gone in the civil-rights plank in the party platform, and, in fact, he did not go quite as far. The platform Senator Goldwater has accepted is, if anything, stronger than President Johnson's. (It urges, as the Democratic one does not, "improvements of civil-rights statutes.") The President was reported—quite erroneously, it developed—to oppose naming the Ku Klux Klan and the John Birch Society in the section on "extremism." And he still seemed to think it possible to make some deal that would avoid alienating either Martin Luther King, Jr., or Bull Connor, the master of the hounds during last year's troubles in Birmingham. Some Eastern Democrats persuaded themselves that the President had discovered a new "consensus," one that was partly reflected in and partly created by the Republicans' nomination of Goldwater. He planned, they feared, to run on all of Goldwater's issues as well as on his own. He would be for war as well as for peace; he would try to get the "white-backlash" vote away from Goldwater by promising more "law and order" in the city streets: he would say "fiscal responsibility" five times for every time Goldwater said it.

These anticipations, on the eve of the convention, seemed far from unreasonable. There seemed little doubt that the rise of Goldwater had been one of the factors, and perhaps the most important one, that determined the timing and magnitude of the military responses he had ordered in the Gulf of Tonkin three weeks earlier. And he had been coupling defenses of his civil-rights positions with gratuitous allusions to the recent eruptions of violence in the Northern cities. But nothing the President said or did here lent any substantial support to the view that Goldwater's candidacy would pull the President several degrees to the right. If the platform language on civil rights has a conciliatory sound, the action of the Credentials Committee in respecting the "moral," as distinct from the legal, claims of the Freedom Democrats was unexpectedly bold. The President may not have welcomed it, but he endorsed it, and in so doing he authorized the introduction of an entirely new element in American party politics. In reversing the right to reject delegates selected by voters whose franchise is an attribute of their race, this convention struck as heavy a blow at "states' rights" as has been struck by any recent legislation or court decision. The Freedom Democrats won a series of victories that not even the most hopeful of their number expected to win five days ago. It is a remarkable and perhaps a historically unprecedented thing that a great national party, firmly in command of governmental power, is making an effort to absorb and give voice to a protest movement that spends much of its energy trying to undermine the party's authority in exactly those places where the authority is most strongly entrenched. Nor was the President deflected from his emphasis on accommodation in foreign policy or from his previously expressed views on the social and economic imperatives of the decade he proposes to dominate. Senator Goldwater had a point when he characterized Johnson's acceptance speech as "isolationist." Read as a document in Cold War history, it has a kind of noninterventionist ring. It proposes no new initiatives except toward disarmament. It boasts of no diplomatic accomplishments except the avoidance of nuclear war. The passages on domestic policy are unashamed defenses of the welfare state and pledges to extend it, with no mentions of "fiscal responsibility." Johnson will try for as much of the Eisenhower vote as he thinks may be within his reach, but if he continues along his present course, the lure will not be agreement with Senator Goldwater but ceaselessly stressed disagreement.

I have said before and I state again here today that this man [Senator Gold-water] is worthy of being included in the list of America's great profiles in courage. . . . I might point out that [on April 30, 1960] he selected me out of all the members of the United States Senate to present him with the annual George Washington Award of the American Good Government Society on that important occasion in his life.

—J. Strom Thurmond, Republican Senator from South Caro-lina, introducing Goldwater at the Greenville airport, September 17, 1964. It was Senator Thurmond's maiden speech as a Republican. The former Demo-crat, who had run for President on the Dixiecrat ticket in 1948, had announced his conversion the night before.

Whether Senator Goldwater himself [was] scared isn't clear, although he later told newsmen the incident had "separated the men from the boys."

—Jack Steele, in the Washington *Daily News*, October 28, 1964. "I know now," Steele wrote, "how it feels to be riding in a 400-mile-an-hour jet airliner diving toward the ground just above the treetops and headed for an inevitable crash. It's not an experience I'd like to repeat. It happened suddenly at Bristol, Tennessee, when Captain Ralph Long, an experienced American Airlines pilot inadvertently [?] scared the living daylights out of forty-five reporters covering Senator Barry M. Goldwater's Presidential cam-paign. [Captain] Long, after a routine takeoff, decided—without warning—to buzz the Tri-Cities airport near Bristol. He wheeled the big jet into a 180-degree turn and swept over the airport runway ground at nearly full speed. Senator Goldwater, a jet pilot himself, jumped from his seat in the plane's forward compartment and rushed to the cockpit when he noticed the plane diving toward the ground. He was quickly reassured by Captain Long. But the reporters riding in the plane's cramped rear section had no such warning. They watched the plane dive earthward until the treetops on the hills sur-rounding the airport were flashing by the windows. Believing a crash was in-evitable, they braced for what many believed would be at least a merciful sudden death."

* A REPORTER AT LARGE AND ALOFT WITH
AND WITHOUT GOLDWATER

September 18, 1964

I spent most of a mid-September week traveling with Senator Goldwater in seven states of the Old Confederacy and in two Border States. Actually, I did not so much travel "with" the Senator as "behind" him. He made his rounds in a Boeing 727, a three-engine jet traveling at very nearly the speed of sound. With him in this plane—the *Yai Bi Ken,* which, according to the candidate, is Navajo for "House in the Sky"—were Mrs. Goldwater, her hairdresser, five or six campaign advisers, and fifty-odd journalists of one sort or another, the majority of whom represented what Goldwater enthusiasts call "the rat-fink Eastern press." * I was part of the journalistic overflow from the *Yai Bi Ken,* some of whose passengers called it the *Enola Gay.* We traveled about—sometimes as many as twelve of us, sometimes as few as five—in a two-engine propeller plane that cruised

* The rat finks picked up the tab. "I'm on a political trip, and the Republican Party is paying for it," Goldwater said in Tulsa early in the campaign, adding that a lot of President Johnson's "political" trips were being paid for by the taxpayers. Goldwater might have gone on to say that while Republican treasurers may be signing the checks for the American Airlines charter, this involves merely a transfer of funds from an account into which newspapers, magazines, and television networks have put thirty-six hundred dollars for each of their representatives traveling with Goldwater. Thus, at the outset of the Campaign, the press gave the Republican National Committee about a quarter of a million dollars to get its campaign, as one might say, off the ground.

at a little better than one-third the speed of the candidate's plane. In theory, we were "following" Goldwater, but this was almost as hopeless as giving hot pursuit to an Alfa Romeo on a tricycle. Thus, we made only about half as many stops as Goldwater did, and it was not uncommon, when we did come out of the skies, to arrive at a rally just as the preacher was saying the benediction, or to leave one after only a few words of the invocation. In Missouri, we never saw Goldwater at all. We landed at the Springfield airport, learned that the motorcade had left for the meeting in town, stopped in at the airport coffee shop for a quick lunch, and took off for Charleston, West Virginia, where, it had been announced, Goldwater was to make a major speech on the administration's antipoverty program. The same thing happened at Macon, Georgia, but there, because of our eagerness to make a rally at the Cramton Bowl, in Montgomery, Alabama, we only had time for a cup of coffee.

All this had its rewards as well as its frustrations. It takes a powerful constitution to endure attendance at eight or ten political rallies a day, and Goldwater rallies in the deep South are, I found, especially taxing. On the whole, I was more relieved than distressed by the news that our group would be unable to make Shreveport, Louisiana, where, according to one authority in our entourage, "there are more haters per square mile than anywhere else in the country." * It was, though, disappointing not to be in Knoxville, Tennessee, to hear Goldwater, standing beneath a rippling Confederate flag, say that he still thought that the TVA, or at least its steam and fertilizer plants, ought to be

---

* I was subsequently advised by a reader that this was an inaccurate and unjust description. She said that the Shreveport Chamber of Commerce had taken the matter up at one of its meetings but had decided against a formal protest because a protest would fall, at the *New Yorker,* on deaf ears. She wished me to know that "Shreveport is a CHRISTIAN city." Perhaps she's right. My only point was that, having got this estimate from a well-known Southern journalist and having seen enough haters in two days to last me through 1964 and well into 1965, I did not raise any freedom-of-the-press issue when told that I could not accompany Goldwater to Shreveport.

sold to private interests, just as it was disappointing to miss his address to senior citizens in Orlando, Florida, on the iniquities of providing hospital care for the aged through the Social Security system.* In any case, the experience, though neither as rich nor as wearing as it might have been, was instructive and in many ways novel. As a fellow traveler, Miss Mary McGrory, of the Washington *Star,* noted, we were undoubtedly the only people who had ever flown from New Orleans to Springfield, Missouri, for lunch—or from Memphis to Macon for a cup of coffee. I don't suppose, either, that anyone before us has ever logged several thousand miles in the South and visited a dozen or so of its great centers of population without seeing any more Negroes than one might expect to encounter on, say, an average winter afternoon in Spitzbergen. Goldwater is the only cicerone who could arrange a trip like that. It was weird. In a Negroless Memphis or Atlanta or New Orleans, many of us had the feeling of having lost our bearings. We would peer out beyond the edges of the crowds and down side streets to see if we could spot a single Negro, and, whenever we saw one, advise one another of our rare discovery. There were novel sounds as well as sights. It has been my lot to attend political gatherings of many sorts since the mid-thirties, but never until I went South with Barry Goldwater had I heard any large number of Americans boo and hoot at the mention of the name of the President of the United States. In Alabama and Louisiana, there were thunderous, stadium-filling boos, all of them cued by a United States Senator.

This Senator is a man easily surprised and endlessly surprising. One of my favorite stories about him—and one of the more agreeable ones—involves the principal of an all-Negro high school in Phoenix back in the days when segregation was the rule

* In his extraordinary postelection interview in *U. S. News & World Report,* December 21, 1964, Goldwater was asked "What do you think now of the issues you raised in the campaign?" He replied, "I wouldn't change my mind on any of them." And he said, when asked specifically about medicare, "I didn't find medicare to be any great issue. In fact, I purposely tried speaking against it in areas where I felt it might be popular. I got very satisfying rounds of applause."

in that city. He once asked Goldwater how it happened that the family department store donated a gold watch as a commencement prize to each of the all-white schools but not to the school he headed. Goldwater replied that he was opposed to segregation and didn't intend to encourage it by supplying an all-Negro school with a prize. The principal replied that, as he viewed the matter, an all-white school was every bit as segregated as an all-Negro school. Goldwater thought this over for a moment or two and then declared, with a delighted grin, that the educator's reasoning was absolutely unassailable. The school got its gold watch. As a ratiocinative being, Goldwater is elated by illuminations of this kind. It may even have pleased him, the other day, to have Walter Lippmann inform him that it hardly makes sense to accuse the President, as Goldwater did in Charleston, of planning an economy in which "no one is permitted to fall below the average," since, in Lippmann's icy words, "there cannot be an 'average' if no one is below it." The Republican candidate's capacity for astonishment is matched by his capacity for astonishing. He is everlastingly outwitting, if that is the word, those who think they know most about him. For two or three years now, quite a number of people, myself among them, have been studying Goldwater and Goldwaterism as intently—and in some cases almost as morbidly—as the Reverend Cotton Mather ever studied the doings of Satan and the manifestations of witchcraft. But not even the most learned and imaginative of Goldwaterologists was prepared for the Senator's emergence, at San Francisco, as a candidate for High Sheriff as well as for President. If Goldwater was anything, he was a states'-rights man, and if there is one states' right, or responsibility, that no one has ever thought of challenging, it is the maintenance of public order and safety and the enforcement of criminal justice. Goldwaterologists in the Cow Palace and across the country were stunned when he proposed to take steps "at the federal level" to "keep the streets safe from bullies and marauders." It was clear enough that talk of this kind would enable him to appeal for the "white-backlash" vote, but it was not clear how, in a lengthy campaign, he could develop this theme without undermining his position as a strict Constitutionalist. A certain amount of order returned to our shattered universe when, shortly after the convention, he was asked how he proposed to deal with questions of implementation. His response was vague—reassuringly vague from our point of view. He said a few words about creating a more exhilarating "moral climate" by force of Presidential example and some about elevating the quality of the federal judiciary. Though still a bit unsettled, we scholars became a bit less uneasy. This, we assumed, was about the size of it—Goldwater would continue to take a stand against "bullies and marauders" (Negro ones, anyway, in the urban jungles above the Mason-Dixon Line) but would not destroy his Constitutional position by proposing any specific strategy of federal intervention. For him, we reasoned, there was more than the Constitution at stake. What is more essential to the Southern way of life than the power of governors over the state troopers, highway patrols, and "public safety" departments? And the Southern fuzz, it was reliably reported, were hot for Goldwater. (I was told that the sight of Goldwater stickers on Southern prowl cars and police motorcycles was not an unusual one. I can myself report having seen only one. This was in Greenville, South Carolina.)

Until the first day of Goldwater's Southern tour, it seemed that the candidate would not go beyond the rhetoric of his acceptance speech and the amplifying statements he made in the days after the convention. But on his first evening out, in a ball park in St. Petersburg, he delivered a speech that went well beyond anything he had said in San Francisco or Phoenix. It was by far the most radical statement he has ever made. In it, he not only undermined his position on the Constitution but threw the document itself away—and the Magna Charta with it. He began by reminding his audience of what he had said in San Francisco and by declaring that it was "a tragedy [that] the breakdown of law and order should be an issue in this campaign for the highest office in the land." But, he went on, "it must be an issue, a major issue," for "the war against crime [is] the only needed war." (So much for South Vietnam—in St. Petersburg, anyway.) He cited a number of alarming statistics on crime (nationwide, he said, it has climbed "five times faster than the population" during the Kennedy-Johnson administration),* and demanded to know how Lyndon Johnson can "ignore the six thousand or so major crimes committed in the last twenty-four hours." (The President was vulnerable enough; like Goldwater, he was in Florida that day, addressing some union machinists in Miami Beach and inspecting the hardware at Cape Kennedy. He didn't do a thing or say so much as a word in sorrow or anger about the last twenty-four hours of crime.) Goldwater then put, in his audience's behalf, the question that had bothered the Goldwaterologists. "How, you will rightly ask, will Bill Miller and I restore domestic tranquillity to the land? Well, let me tell you how we will do it." It cannot be reported that the audience quivered with anticipation; there is, if anything, rather a surfeit of domestic tranquillity in St. Petersburg, which is still, despite Einstein and the population explosion, the town celebrated in Ring Lardner's "The Golden Honeymoon." But Goldwater went on. In essence, what he and Bill Miller would do to

---

* Throughout the campaign Goldwater was partial to nationwide statistics, though he now and then cited as particularly disgraceful Washington and New York where, of course, a large number of felons are Negroes. He never got around to any mention of Phoenix, which has the fourth-highest crime rate in the country. (Washington is thirteenth.) In the *New Republic* for October 3, James Ridgway had some comparative figures: "Goldwater talks about Washington, where Negroes account for some 54 percent of the population; but in Goldwater's own town of Phoenix, where the population is 95 percent white, the crime rate is a third higher than in Washington. Moreover, during the first six months of this year, crime in the suburbs—where few Negroes dwell—went up 28 percent; crime in the cities increased by half that rate. A city such as New York, where there was a good deal of civil-rights agitation, had a lower rate than Los Angeles, which had fewer demonstrations. Philadelphia, long plagued with Negro unrest, has a relatively low crime rate among larger cities. The three highest centers of crime, ahead of Phoenix, are Las Vegas, Los Angeles, and Miami."

combat lawlessness would be to change the law or ignore it. In the first place, they would appoint judges who understand, as they do, that the important thing about law enforcement was to get the offenders off the streets and behind bars. When the law, as understood by the courts of appeal, got in the way of prosecutors, the law should be either revised or overlooked. "Something must be done," Goldwater said, "and done right away, to swing away from this obsessive concern for the rights of the criminal defendant." He gave some examples of the "obsessive concern," all of which were Supreme Court rulings intended to observe the due-process clause and the rights set forth in the Fourth, Fifth, Sixth, Seventh, and Eighth Amendments to the Constitution of the United States. It was nonsense, Goldwater said, for the Supreme Court to hold a confession inadmissible merely because a defendant did not have his lawyer's advice at the time he made it; the only point is whether the confession was a recital of the truth. He said that he and Miller would urge upon Congress a statute voiding the Mallory ruling, which, as summarized by him, "holds that any statement made by a defendant to police officers is inadmissible if arraignment is delayed." If he had said that the Constitution is a lot of ink on paper, he would have described it about as adequately as he described the Mallory ruling in St. Petersburg. The ruling, made in 1957 for the District of Columbia, deals at some length with the appropriate limits of prearraignment examination of a suspect and with the question of how much time is enough and how much is too much between arrest and arraignment. Washington policemen are unhappy with it, and so is Goldwater. About it, and about other manifestations of the "obsessive concern" with the rights of defendants, Goldwater would, he said, do two things. He would, "in making appointments to the federal judiciary, [consider] the need to redress Constitutional interpretation in favor of the public." And, as insurance in the event that court-packing didn't work, he would support a Constitutional amendment to "give back to the states those powers absolutely needed for fair and efficient administration of criminal law." If the amendment embodied his present view of what "powers" the states need, it would effectively repeal about half the Bill of Rights. "In your hearts," he said, "you know there must be a change. And in your hearts you know that Bill Miller and I will be that change."

The crowd at Al Lang Field in St. Petersburg was, like most of Goldwater's Southern crowds, good-sized, enthusiastic, and responsive more to his presence than to his words. It is, of course, axiomatic that political crowds are more interested in seeing than in listening, and most candidates nowadays give the live audience their material presence and direct their words to radio and television audiences and to readers of newspapers. But in this, as in so many other matters, things have always been a bit different in the South. Its masses have always relished strong, vivid political rhetoric. They will travel long distances to hear it, and, other things being equal or even a little unequal, reward eloquence at the polls. Goldwater nowhere attempted to satisfy the Southern appetite for language. The lines he got from his writers were as flat as his delivery of them. Even when the substance was inflammatory, the form was soporific: statistics on crime, discussions of previously unheard-of Supreme Court rulings and internal-security cases, arguments over the relative merits of defense contractors. But this rarely dampened the enthusiasm the crowds had brought with them to the gatherings. The quality of this enthusiasm, one felt, was essentially nonpolitical. These were not really *political* rallies—they were revels, they were pageants, they were celebrations. The aim of the revelers was not so much to advance a candidacy or a cause as to dramatize a mood. The mood was a kind of joyful defiance, or defiant joy. By coming south, Barry Goldwater had made it possible for great numbers of unapologetic white supremacists to hold great carnivals of white supremacy. They were not troubled in the least over whether this would hurt the Republican Party in the rest of the country; they wanted to make— for their own satisfaction, if for no one else's—a display of the fact that they had found, and were enjoying membership in, one organization that was secure against integration because it had made itself secure against Negro aspirations. As long as they could put on shows of this kind, no Negro would ever want in. By far the most memorable of the shows was staged in Cramton Bowl, a few miles outside Montgomery, Alabama, on Goldwater's second night out. Some unsung Alabama Republican had hit upon an idea of breathtaking simplicity—to show the country the "lily-white" character of Republicanism in Dixie by planting, for the Goldwater rally in the bowl, a great field of white lilies—living lilies, in perfect bloom, gorgeously arrayed. The night was soft; the stars and the moon were bright; the grass in the bowl was impossibly green, as if it grew out of something far richer than dirt; the stadium lights did not destroy the colors and shadows of evening, but they lighted the turf so individual blades of grass could be seen. And sown on the turf were seven hundred Alabama girls in long white gowns, all of a whiteness as impossible as the greenness of the green. The girls came, we were told, from every one of Alabama's sixty-seven counties— from Tallapoosa and Bibb and Etowah and Coffee—as well as from Montgomery, Birmingham, and Mobile. Their dresses were uniform only in color and length; taken all in all it was a triumph, among other things, of Alabama couture.

The sowing of lilies had been done about a half hour before the proceedings were to begin. The girls stood on the turf, each waving a small American flag, while the bands played and the arrangers made and announced last-minute arrangements. Then, right on schedule, an especially powerful light played on a stadium gate at about the fifty-yard line, and the candidate of the Republican Party rode in as slowly as a car can be made to go, first down past fifty or so yards of choice Southern womanhood, and then, after a sharp left at the goal line, past more girls to the gorgeously draped stand. It was all as solemn and as stylized as a review of troops by some such master of the art as General de Gaulle. The girls did not behave like troops—they swayed a bit as Goldwater passed, and sounds came from them—not squeals or shrieks, but pleasing and ladylike murmurs. And in a sense, of course, they *were* Goldwater's troops, as well as representatives of what the rest of his Southern troops—the thousands in the packed stands, the tens of thousands in Memphis and New Orleans and Atlanta and Shreveport and Greenville—passionately believed they were defending. When at last he mounted the platform, the lilies departed the gridiron and arranged themselves on the sidelines. There they listened to what was by far the limpest speech Goldwater delivered anywhere in the South. It wasn't about anything in particular. He said that big government was bad and that he and Bill Miller proposed to put an end to it, though not right away. ("Because of existing commitments, we cannot do this overnight. But we can gradually replace this undesirable and complex system with a much simpler and more sensible one [without] making dangerous cuts in national defense or in necessary domestic programs.") The crowd loved it. It may even have been relieved that the speech was low in key and did not drive out memories of the spectacle that had preceded it.

Though one saw little evidence of it at the Goldwater pageants and picnics, the South has more on its mind than race. Opinion polls show the region as a whole just about evenly split between the candidates. Goldwater cannot lose Alabama, where the President will not be on the ballot, and he should have no trouble winning Mississippi, whose Democratic organization has put up a slate of Johnson electors and urged everyone to vote against them. It would surprise most experts if Johnson won Louisiana, where Goldwater has more billboard space than Ford, Chrysler, and General Motors; it would also surprise them if the President lost Arkansas, North Carolina, Virginia, and Texas. But in most places the division is expected to be close. There are, plainly, large numbers of Southerners—white Southerners—who will cast their votes on issues other than race. In August, Representative Charles Bass, of Tennessee, the only Southern Democrat to vote for the civil-rights bill, easily won a nomination for the Senate against a segregationist. In a late September primary Representative Harry Wingate, Jr., of Georgia, the one Democrat Goldwater endorsed on the Southern tour, lost his seat, in a district said to be full of racists of the most benighted sort, to a man supporting the national administration. A former Goldwater Democrat, Senator Thurmond, of South Carolina, made his first appearance as a Goldwater Republican at the candidate's side in Greenville, and the man who introduced him to the airport picnickers there said that Thurmond's decision of the day before had been as notable an event in Southern history as Robert E. Lee's decision to resign his commission in the United States Army for a command in the Army of Northern Virginia. Thurmond's defection was undoubtedly an event to be noted; it gladdened the party he left and saddened the party he joined, which can no longer boast that it has no racists in high elective office. Southern politicians do not believe that Thurmond joined the Republicans because he thought the Party had a bright future in South Carolina; he crossed over, they think, because he would not, in all probability, have been renominated as a Democrat in 1966, when he is due to be opposed by the incumbent governor, Donald S. Russell.

Still, the Goldwater movement, whether or not it can command a majority, remains an enormous one in the South and appears to be a racist movement and very little else. Goldwater seemed fully aware of this and not visibly distressed by it. He did not, to be sure, make any direct racist appeals. He covered the South and never, in any public gatherings, mentioned "race" or "Negroes" or "whites" or "segregation" or "civil rights." But the fact that the words did not cross his lips does not mean that he ignored the realities they describe. He talked about them all the time in an underground, or Aesopian, language—a kind of code that few in his audiences had any trouble deciphering. In the code, "bullies and marauders" means "Negroes." "Criminal defendants" means "Negroes." "States' rights" means "opposition to civil rights." "Women" means "white women." This much of the code is as easily understood by his Northern audiences as by his Southern ones, but there are words that have a more limited and specific meaning for the Southern crowds. Thus, in the

Old Confederacy, "Lyndon Baines Johnson" and "my opponent" mean "integrationist." "Hubert Horatio" (it somehow amuses Goldwater to drop the "Humphrey") means "super-integration-ist." "Federal judiciary" means "integrationist judges." It would be going too far to say that he touched Southern sensibilities on race when he brought up Bobby Baker, the TFX controversy, fiscal policy, or "Yo-yo" McNamara. He certainly was not arous-ing them when he talked of TVA in Knoxville and medicare in Orlando. One had always the feeling, though, that the Goldwater Republicans in the South could find a racial or regional angle in almost anything. When Bobby Baker, a Pickens, South Caro-lina, man, who once enjoyed a friendly relationship with Senator Thurmond, was hooted at Goldwater meetings (as he was every-where, except in Greenville, where delicacy prevailed and he was not mentioned), it was not because the speaker was deploring Baker's activities in business and politics. It was because of his embarrassing connections with the integrationist in the White House. And Goldwater generally played it that way. He would rattle off some figures on murders, rapes, and muggings, and then explain that "nothing is more clear from history than that the moral decay of a people begins at the top," following this with a quick mention of Bobby Baker, as if Bobby Baker was some kind of hoodlum lieutenant and riot organizer rather than a conspicuously successful entrepreneur. Among Goldwater Southerners, even thermonuclear warfare gets identified with regional pride, sentiment, and rancor. An Atlanta matron, be-decked with Goldwater-Miller buttons, was asked if she had ever been disturbed by things the candidate had said about war and weaponry. "Certainly not," she replied. "We're not cowards down here."

In the South, as elsewhere, Goldwater attacked the President for having so inadequate an appreciation of the "Communist menace" that he had never mentioned it in his Atlantic City ac-ceptance speech. And two or three times he taxed the administra-tion with negligence with Communist subversion in this country. Up to now, though, internal security and domestic Communism have been distinctly minor themes in the campaign, and this, too, has been a surprise to Goldwaterologists, who were certain that in due time a generous amount of McCarthyism would be stirred in the Goldwater brew. The hard core of Goldwater's support has always come from people whose alarm centers on Communists in the United States and who tend to relate, and subordinate, all other issues to this one. The only other leader these people have had in recent times was the late Joseph R. McCarthy, and while McCarthy lived, Goldwater followed and championed him. Goldwater voted against McCarthy's censure by the Senate, and shortly after McCarthy's death went to Wisconsin to tell a Republican state convention there that "Because Joe McCarthy lived, we are a safer, freer, more vigilant nation today. This fact, even though he no longer dwells among us, will never perish." McCarthy has not been mentioned in the campaign, though, and McCarthy's strategies have not been employed, except now and then by Congressman Miller, and not even Miller has accused anyone of treason. Pay dirt, it would seem, is being overlooked. The Johnson administration is filled with people McCarthy called traitors. Moreover, there now seems little doubt that Communists, particularly those whose sympathies are more with Peking than with Moscow, have had a hand in provoking racial disorders in the Northern cities and have infiltrated some civil-rights organizations. And in those Northern working-class districts where the "white backlash" is said to be a fact of political life, there are many people of Eastern European origin who are more receptive than most to the argument that anything evil or distressing must be Communist in origin.

There was a moment during the Southern tour that seemed made to order for a revival of McCarthyism. Early on the morning of the last day in the South, Goldwater flew from New Orleans to Longview, Texas, for an airport rally, where the candidate was to be presented by the Honorable Martin L. Dies, a former congressman from Texas. Dies was the architect of the House Committee on Un-American Activities. He was the John the Baptist of McCarthyism. There was once a time, in the late thirties and early forties, when liberals and radicals, and more than a few conservatives, would blanch at the mention of his name. His committee once solemnly declared that Shirley Temple, then a recent alumna of a Hollywood kindergarten and a child actress whose performances dampened handkerchiefs all around the world, was a stooge of the Stalinists. Now an attorney in private practice, this lifelong Democrat and scourge of subversives had come out of political retirement to introduce Barry Goldwater in his maiden appearance, as a Presidential candidate, in Texas. And it was to be an all-star show—not only Goldwater and Dies but J. Strom Thurmond (once aboard, he seemed impossible to lose; he stayed with Goldwater until the campaign headed north) and "the Little Giant of Texas," Senator John Tower. The airport crowd—respectable in size, overwhelming in ardor—was ready for a resurgence of McCarthyism. But the men on the platform were not. Senator Thurmond, who introduced Dies, was so out of tune with history that he couldn't pronounce the great Texan's name, once a household word, properly. It rhymes with "cries," but as Thurmond had it, it was "Die-ease." And then Martin Dies arose and, without a mention of Communist termites, said he was honored to introduce Goldwater, who mumbled a few words about some work of a Paul Revere type that Dies had once, long ago, done and followed these with his "basic" speech: "When you woke up on a typical morning of this administration, Lyndon's day of spending was just beginning. And by the evening, when his day of spending was complete, he would have spent ten million dollars more than his predecessor spent. . . . While we talk, every four minutes frugal Lyndon puts another person on the public payroll."

When the meeting was over, I asked Dies if he intended to follow Thurmond's lead and switch parties. The forerunner of McCarthy looked at me as though I had asked a question of utter madness. "I just *introduced* Goldwater," he said. "I'm *voting* the Democratic ticket."

Goldwater's failure to exploit the Communist issue may be a mere oversight—oversights have been numerous in this campaign—or it may be symptomatic of an atmospheric change of some importance. Among Goldwater zealots, what one hears when one expects to hear "Communist" or "subversive" is "Easterner" or "liberal." Until a few years ago, it would have been difficult—indeed, it would have been impossible—to provoke pungent expressions of disapprobation simply by identifying a critic or antagonist as an "Eastern liberal." In some regions, "Eastern" had certain disagreeable associations—of slickness, snobbishness, pretense—but a man was not suspect merely because he lived north of Washington and east of Pittsburgh. In some quarters, the word "liberal" was pejorative; the overtones, though, were not of wickedness but of softness, gullibility, insufficient reverence. No man exposed himself to contumely simply by acknowledging that he was from the East or by describing himself as liberal in persuasion. Before he could be condemned, it was necessary to implicate him in something inherently diabolical. He had, as a rule, to be called a secret Communist or a dupe of Communists or, in McCarthy's phrase for members of the Senate who opposed him, a "handmaiden of Communism." But in recent years, under the tutelage of Goldwater and other rightists, large numbers of Americans have gone far beyond this. In Goldwater circles, an Easterner is guilty until he proves himself innocent. There is no longer a need to identify a liberal with Communism. It is quite bad enough if he is a "liberal," doubly bad if he is an "Eastern liberal." In a sense, it is worse to be a liberal from the East than to be a Communist from anywhere. Communists at least command respect and emulation. Goldwaterites do not suggest that the "Eastern press" is Communist in sympathy. It is enough for them that it is Eastern and, in their view, predominantly "liberal." The code word for it is not "Communist" but "liars." The "Eastern Establishment" is not held to be a Communist front; it is simply the "Eastern Establishment," and no more need be said to draw catcalls. Its headquarters, of course, are in New York. I was given, for purposes of identification, a badge on which the name of the *New Yorker,* minus the definite article, was lettered, large and clear and black. Life would have been far easier, among Goldwater crowds in the South, if it had said "LEPER." I declined to wear it after being asked, for the sixth time, how things were in Harlem.

There were times, traveling with Goldwater, when one wondered whether the candidate really thinks of himself as a man seeking the Presidency of the United States. No doubt the answer is that he does. It seems unlikely that he would go around the South agitating the most brazen of its racists if he did not think this means was justified by some noble end. Still, the whole enterprise has the air not of a great political campaign but of a great political caper—a series of pranks and calculated errors. Unless all the rules have been suspended for this year, unless Barry Goldwater knows something that Republican leaders in New York and Pennsylvania and Michigan and Illinois and Ohio and even Georgia and Florida and Texas do not know, the entire strategy is a joke. Goldwater keeps saying that he does know something others don't know, but he can't quite tell what it is. In one town after another, beginning long before the Southern tour, he has been telling his audiences that "Bill Miller and I know there is something stirring in this country, something just below the surface." He goes on to say that "we can't put our finger on it at the moment, but I think that in a week or ten days we'll be able to describe it pretty accurately." Almost four weeks have gone by since he first said this publicly (he was saying it before in off-the-record press conferences), and the puzzle remains unsolved. Presumably he feels that there are some special conditions that make what his advisers call "the Southern strategy"—using the South's electoral votes as the foundation of victory—peculiarly valid in 1964. Perhaps he is right, but politicians of far greater experience than his think that "the Southern strategy" was never less valid than in 1964. Right or wrong, he seemed to be under some compulsion to damage his own cause even in the South. He talked against TVA in the TVA country and against medicare in the medicare country. He delivered his extraordinary "law and order" speech in St. Petersburg, the most lawabiding of communities. He attacked legislative reapportionment in Atlanta, a city which has maintained the largest reapportionment lobby in Washington, and then went outside Atlanta to attack it again in a brand-new congressional district born of reapportionment. Asked to explain this unusual political behavior, his spokesmen said the Senator was a man of courage and forthrightness; he would rather be right than popular. Other explanations, however, were in order for his reluctance to say anything that would upset the racists.

He ended the first Southern tour with the rally in Longview, where he cast a bit more light on questions of strategy by saying, "I do not intend to go around the country discussing complicated, twisted issues." That evening, making a Northern re-entry by way of Charleston, West Virginia, he said, "The task of the true statesman, said Aristotle, is to see dangers from afar. Now, I do not claim to be a statesman." In the capital of Appalachia, he unburdened himself of some thoughts on poverty. The President's program was, he said, "phony." Poverty was as much a state of mind as anything else. It was also a verbal and statistical trick, put across by economists who simply "redefined the luxuries of yesterday as the necessities of today." He said the administration was compelling people to think poor. "If someone who ought to feel deprived [for lack of yesterday's luxuries] doesn't respond that way, some politician in my opponent's curious camp—perhaps the leader himself—will drive up to his door to see to it that he feels the way he ought." He pointed out that people in Pakistan are much poorer than Americans. The living standards of the American "poor"—in the written text of his speeches, the word is always in quotation marks—"represent material well-being beyond the dreams of a vast majority of the people of the world outside these United States." In an elegant ad-libbed section on the origins of the capitalist system, he said he thought it really started when some "smart ape" began setting aside coconuts fallen from trees and selling them to other "apes," some of whom lacked the spirit of enterprise and became resentful at having to buy what formerly was a bounty of nature. He thought the President's views on the economy "dreadful," because they provided "no penalty for failure." "In your hearts, you know this is so." He conceded that there was some problem about unemployed youth and school dropouts. But the administration's retraining program was no fit solution. For one thing, it would, he said, "cost ten thousand dollars for each recruit." He had a money-saving plan. "It would be cheaper to give them four years of education in your own fine state university, where they would learn a lot more." He did not linger on the problems that such a solution might pose for American higher education.

I have never seen as grim and uncomprehending a group of politicians as those West Virginia Republicans who sat on the platform with Goldwater in Charleston. They joined in two bursts of applause—once when he mentioned the Ten Commandments, and again when he said, "We will not convert the heathen by losing our own souls."

Y'all come on down to the speaking.

> —President Johnson, addressing street crowds through a bull horn as his motorcade made its way toward the center of a hundred American cities in the fall of 1964

I left Washington early this morning. I have been going all day long. I am going to continue to go until November 3rd. On Election night I am going to be at my little ranch home on the banks of the Pedernales down the road from where my mother, my father, my grandmother, my grandfather, my great-grandfather, and great-grandmother are buried, and I am going to be waiting until we hear from the great state of Illinois [elsewhere, Ohio, Indiana, Tennessee, etc.]. I think I know what I am going to hear if you don't let me down. We are going to get the job done, and we are going to do it up brown.

> —President Johnson, at the "speaking," here, there, and everywhere

October 1964

Early this month, I spent several days in the Middle West and the Upper South observing President Johnson as he campaigned in municipal plazas and on street corners, in auditoriums large and small, in banquet halls elegant and shabby, at airports and parking lots, on public-school playgrounds and university campuses. It was his first sustained tour, and the first in which he acknowledged that he was doing "political business" and no other kind. Everywhere he went, he appealed to Democrats, Republicans, and all other enfranchised Americans to put aside their differences, abide by the Golden Rule, and keep him on in the White House, where, he said, he could be counted upon to do "anything that is honorable" in order to avoid "mashing that button that will blow up the world." He would, he said, "pick up the phone" whenever it rang at his end of the "hot line"* and commend to Khrushchev, or whoever else was calling, the late Sam Rayburn's first rule of statesmanship: "Just a minute—let's have a look at this and think it through." There were times on this trip when one could not avoid speculating as to what might happen if the "hot line" chanced to be ringing, or chattering, at the moment. The crowds had torn the antennas from the rolling bomb shelter that has been made, according

* Political (and journalistic) license. The "hot line" runs not between telephones, but between teletype machines. Communication is by written messages rather than voice.

153

to Secret Service specifications, of the Lincoln Continental in which John F. Kennedy died, and as often as not Lyndon Johnson, to the horror of local policemen, was far out in the crowd, working it like a popcorn vendor seized with a mad passion to make a fortune in a day. There were times, too, when it seemed as if he were determined to render himself physically incapable of "mashing" anything or of lifting a phone from its cradle. Human hands have seldom taken such punishment as his have taken in recent weeks. He apparently wants to turn the entire United States into one great transcontinental reception line. Several hours of each working day are devoted to clutching the hands of all within shaking distance. His boarding-house reach enables him to make it over three or four bodies for midair rendezvous with the upstretched hands of well-wishers. Those whose hands cannot connect with his may find his fingers lightly touching their scalps or their shoulders—or at least fluttering close to their eyes. Where crowds are kept behind barriers (a restraint on liberty that he seems to deplore and may someday abolish), he covers about a hundred yards of crushed humanity in a little over a minute—with a grip and a smile and now and then a word for those who came early enough to make the first few rows, and with a faith healer's touch for the slugabeds toward the rear. I have seen him with four hands in his own right one and another four in his left.

He wishes to shake even the hand that is not proffered. On a dark, raw night, at the airport in Louisville, I stood behind a line of eminent Kentucky Democrats who had come out to greet him as he deplaned from Air Force One. My eyes and ears were absorbed by the rite I was witnessing, and my hands were enjoying the relative warmth of my topcoat pockets when, of a sudden, a long Presidential arm shot toward me, removed my right hand from my right pocket, clasped it, and returned it to me. Kentucky Democrats are a feuding lot, and he could have thought, seeing me as I stood back in the shadows, that I was some kind of dissident who might be brought into line by his friendly gesture. I doubt, though, that he had time for such reasoning. I rather think that the gesture was purely reflexive—one conditioned by the conviction that no hand could possibly have a good reason for secluding itself when a President's eager, affectionate hand is near. Bruises, swellings, and lacerations are the price he pays for this and related convictions. At each day's end, which is generally the next day's beginning, late callers are treated to a display of the stigmata not yet concealed by bandages. They signify, though, not suffering or sacrifice, but accomplishment.

His quest is for votes. He would like about seventy million of them from the people and five hundred and thirty-eight from the Electoral College. It has been suggested that if he learned on the morning of November 4 that he had lost ten states, he might decline to serve, saying that he just didn't want to be President unless he could be President of *all* the people. The jest says something about his temperament if not about his character. He delights in large crowds because he sees in them a large popular vote. The reasoning may be faulty—though it is hard to find wherein it may be flawed when at a place like Springfield, Illinois (population 83,000, and largely Republican), one of many stops in a crowded day, he saw twenty-five thousand people, or more than Barry Goldwater encountered on a whole day of campaigning in New Jersey. Johnson though, does not measure success merely by the size of the turnouts and the evidence of political approval he finds in the estimates. He is eager to demonstrate to others and perhaps to himself that he has with the masses of the American people what he has lately taken to describing as "rapport," a word that has often been used in articles and speeches as describing something he lacks. It is said that he is short on charisma and has yet to win a large, secure place in the hearts of his countrymen. Scholars, journalists, clergymen, and fellow-politicians have compared his standing among the people with that of Dwight Eisenhower, John Kennedy, and others, and the comparisons have seldom favored Lyndon Johnson. He has found this displeasing, and one of his purposes is to see to it that more favorable comparisons will henceforth be drawn. To this end, he has not been above contriving the kind of display he wants. No determined candidate is ever above this kind of contrivance, and on the score of determination no candidate has ever surpassed this one. Orders go out from the White House to deliver bodies for rallies as well as votes for election—and the bodies are to be happy, full-throated, placard-bearing vessels. The President, the mastermind of his own campaign, is attentive to details of every kind. Impressed by the effect created—on him, at least—by placards crudely hand-lettered with slogans coined by their makers ("TWENTY PERCENT FEWER CAVITIES WITH JOHNSON" and "SELL TVA? I'D SOONER SELL ARIZONA"), he recently, according to the sworn deposition of an eavesdropping correspondent, instructed an assistant to "get a lot more of those homemade signs made."

No amount of contrivance, however, could bring out the kind of crowds he was getting when I traveled with him. The best that the best of politicians can do is to round up the city-hall and courthouse hangers-on and pensioners, their friends and families, and the schoolchildren whose teachers and principals have been persuaded—with perhaps a little talk about bond issues and the need for higher salaries—that seeing a President or a Presidential candidate is a civics lesson in itself. Pressure can bring out the nucleus of a crowd, but not a true crowd. The Johnson crowds I have seen have been gigantic—often totaling, by the most skeptical of estimates, better than 50 per cent of the population center in which they have formed. (The estimate accepted by most newspapers for Des Moines, with a population of two hundred and nine thousand, was one hundred and seventy-five thousand.) By almost all indexes of support and enthusiasm of which I am aware, they measured up to any crowds I have ever seen. Patently, the sight of Lyndon Johnson does not produce the raptures in teen-age girls that the sight of his predecessor produced four years ago. He is, after all, a father figure, as Eisenhower was, as General de Gaulle is, and those who respond to him seem to want his approval and to hear his counsel. They give him their own approval even when he appears to be scolding and giving orders, when he is telling them it is time to "quit our big talk and our bragging" and get on with the serious business of electing "Lyndon Johnson and Hubert Humphrey by the greatest landslide." From all outward appearances, he has as much "rapport" as any candidate in the postwar period. And he is determined that everyone shall believe this and spread word of it. Once, after he had already gone the length of a screaming crowd behind an airport fence, he spotted a journalist who had lately expressed doubt about the popular esteem in which the President was held. "Come over here," he said. "I saw what you wrote about my not having rapport, and now I'm just going to show you something." With the journalist at his side, he went back to the roaring crowd, allowed his hand to be mangled a bit more, and said, "Now, how about that?"

It is generally considered good form for incumbent Presidents to campaign from the White House. They can get as much publicity there as they can get touring the provinces, and the electorate, it is believed, feels that a sitting President ought to sit. For a time, in late summer, the word from the White House was that Johnson planned very little in the way of active campaigning. He would attend to pressing affairs of state and let that indefatigable talker Hubert Humphrey do most of the talking for the Democratic side. Now he has mounted a traveling campaign of unparalleled ferocity. Kennedy worked long hours in 1960, talked himself hoarse day after day, and often went to bed with aching, bloody hands. It was an impressive performance, but not as impressive as Johnson's. Kennedy flew about in the family Convair, which in any given period of time was able to cover only about a third the distance that Johnson covers in the Presidential Boeing 707. Kennedy's handshaking was mainly done where the clusters of humanity were small and reasonably manageable—picnickers along the road, children turned out from country schools, families out to watch at minor traffic intersections. Johnson plunges into whopping, surging, frightening crowds. A half-hour speech was an uncommonly long one for Kennedy. Johnson's are rarely that short, and he now and then runs on, almost in the Latin manner, for an hour and a half. He is campaigning as if he were an almost hopeless underdog—an attitude that leads his traveling companions to shudder at the thought of what lengths he might go to, what prodigies of combat he might perform if he actually believed himself to be behind Barry Goldwater. He does not in fact believe anything of the sort. Although he occasionally warns of the perils of overconfidence, he more often talks as if an enormous victory were assured, as if the only remaining questions were the magnitude of the impending triumph and the uses to which it should be put. He wants it to be as large as possible, but this does not altogether explain his present behavior. He can have little reason for thinking that he is really broadening the base of his support by turning up everywhere; the most he is doing is demonstrating how broad it already is. But that demonstration, according to him, is most effectively made in the opinion polls he is always feasting his eyes on (in the White House, he has them graphically translated into bright-colored charts on huge pieces of pasteboard) and is pleased to discuss with every friendly visitor. The victory he hopes to duplicate—Franklin Roosevelt's re-election in 1936—was won at very little cost in Presidential energy.

No doubt the explanation lies partly in his desire to confound his critics and display, to their chagrin and his own gratification, his "rapport" with the people. Partly, too, it may lie in a feeling of political deprivation. He did not win the Presidency but inherited it, and now he wishes not only to be elected in his own right but also to experience for himself the transports of a national campaign. Harry Truman may have felt something of the sort as he prepared to stump the country in 1948, but Truman, of course, had more compelling reasons for taking to the road. His party was split; there were defections on his left, to Henry A. Wallace, and on his right, to J. Strom Thurmond, and the polls showed him running behind Thomas E. Dewey. Whatever the case may be, Johnson's campaign is reminiscent

SUGAR AND SALT

more of Harry Truman's than of any other within memory. The resemblances between the two men are mainly superficial in character. Johnson is an infinitely more complicated man than Truman; his political instincts are surer and subtler than Truman's ever were, and are informed by light-years more experience and accumulated knowledge. Where Truman was blunt, Johnson is cunning. Truman is an authentic provincial, while Johnson is a worldling who sometimes masquerades as a rustic. But both have back-country manners, and each can claim, as could no one else who has sought the Presidency in the last three decades, to be a true man of the people. For this campaign, at least in the parts of it I recently observed, the Johnson who is capable of being deeply hurt by complaints that he lacks John Kennedy's "style" has shucked his enormous sophistication to make the kind of homely appeals that Truman made in 1948. At times, even the language of the Truman campaign is echoed. "I don't want you to vote for me," Truman was saying sixteen years ago, at county seats and railroad division points all across the country. "I want you to get out on Election Day and vote for yourselves. Vote for your own interests, your own part of the country, your own friends." It seemed at the time a rather parochial approach for a man who, as sponsor of the Marshall Plan and a number of other schemes for postwar recovery, had a large claim to recognition as a world statesman, but he made it anyway, and it worked—or, at any rate, it seemed to work— and Lyndon Johnson is making it now. "Don't you vote for Grandpa or Brother-in-law or anything else," he says. "You vote for yourself. And get your friends and your uncles and your cousins and your aunts to the polls to elect Lyndon Johnson and Hubert Humphrey."

"Don't let them take it away!" was Truman's cry, and it is Johnson's, too. "Is there anyone here," he asks his audiences, "who really wants to shift the gears now, to go into reverse? No, I don't propose to do away with Social Security. And I don't intend to make it voluntary. I want to keep it, and I want to keep all the other good things. And I want all of you to carry this message to the people. They have to know that all these things that they believe in, all these things that they fought for, all these things that they treasure and that they want to pass on to their children so that they can have a better life than they have had—they have to know that they can all go down the drain on November 3rd if you just sit in your rocking chair at home and don't vote." Johnson's manner, when he is on tour and speaking to local audiences, differs from Truman's mainly in his treatment of his opponents. Truman followed to the letter his friends' suggestion to "give 'em hell, Harry." To him, all Republicans were "mossbacks," and he never spoke of the national legislature, which was then dominated by Republicans, as anything but "that good-for-nothing, do-nothing Republican Eightieth Congress." Johnson, who would like to be an ecumenical President, unfailingly takes the line that he has at heart the best interests of all Republicans as well as of all Democrats and, as he sometimes puts it, of all the "whatnots." Of his opponent as an individual, he speaks in friendly terms—"I think well of him"—and of those around Goldwater he will say no more than "Some of them are pretty tense people. Some of them have blood in their eyes. They're impulsive." It seems, in the circumstances, quite enough to say, since there is nothing about himself that he is more eager to prove than that he is calm, clear-eyed, circumspect, and incapable—as he implausibly maintains all other Americans are—of hatred. "We're a nation of lovers," he says in almost every speech. And "We know we're not going to win for America by talking about each other, and using a lot of ugly names, and slinging a lot of mud, and chewing on each other." In Indianapolis, he made an impassioned impromptu plea for Christian forbearance and forgiveness, saying, "Let's try to find the areas which can unite America instead of the few, petty things that divide us. Let's teach our children to love thy neighbor instead of hate each other, and let's say to those men of little faith—let's say to those who are distressed and those who are frustrated and those who are bitter—'Let's turn the other cheek.' Let's look up there and say, 'God, forgive them, for they know not what they do.' " With a bloody hand, he directed the attention of the crowd to the spire of Christ Church Cathedral.

An incumbent President has many advantages, but one advantage his opponent invariably has is in the selection of campaign issues. In theory, the administration's record is always the principal matter under discussion, but an administration's record is never one thing but many, and the challenging candidate can usually decide what in the record will be discussed. In foreign policy, Johnson has taken the play from Goldwater and made "nuclear responsibility" the largest issue—or, at least, the issue that seems to be the largest one presently in the minds of American voters. But it is Goldwater who has decided what domestic matters shall be discussed. The President reported accurately on Goldwater's decision when, in a speech in Cleveland, he said, "The issue in our domestic affairs is whether the whole course of American development up to this time is right or wrong," and he went on to say, "I am just going to visit with you like you were home folks, and I am going to talk with you a few minutes about this domestic issue." The "few minutes" turned out to be approximately sixty, and he offered, as he had said he would, a defense of Social Security, the TVA, minimum-wage laws, the Federal Deposit Insurance Corporation, the United States Housing Authority, the Wagner Act, the Securities and Exchange Commission, the Employment Act of 1946, the G.I. Bill of Rights, the Civil Rights Act of 1964, and the Kennedy-Johnson tax program. Goldwater is not on record in opposition to all of these, but they were all part of the record he is challenging. The President's defense of them was spirited but hardly stimulating and, except perhaps on civil rights and taxes, wildly irrelevant. He put in another half hour defending his favorable view of "nuclear responsibility," which was "relevant," all right, but which in a saner time would seem a needless assurance from a President of the United States. He rambled on about it anyway, made his point, and got back to domestic affairs—the Area Redevelopment Act, the Manpower Act, the Trade

Expansion Act—and then, close to the end of a seemingly endless evening, said, with what at the time seemed brilliant clarity, "I regret one thing deeply, and that is that this senseless argument about what has already been decided defeats what ought to be the purpose of this campaign. This campaign's purpose is to decide what our course is for the future. The argument shouldn't be between the present and the past. The argument ought to be about the present and the future." It was good to know that he, too, wished he were playing in a better show.

. . . the biggest faker in the U.S.A.

—Goldwater, on the President of the United States, San Francisco, July 14

We're for Molly and the babies.

—President Johnson, in many speeches. It was not clear whether "Molly" was chosen because of a Presidential memory of "My Blue Heaven," a popular song of the thirties, in which a refrain ran, "Just Molly and me/ And baby makes three . . . in my blue heaven."

* A SEASON FOR SIMPLE ANSWERS: REFLECTIONS ON THE EVE

November 1, 1964

Presidential campaigns tend on the whole to demean the candidates, diminish the Presidency, and debase the currency of political discourse. It is tempting to say that the one now ending broke all records for unpleasantness and was the most spectacularly unedifying display of its kind in this century. Perhaps it was, as everyone seems to be saying, the worst. We must, though, recall some impressive precedents. The campaign of 1952, for example, featured leading men of sober mien and rather gentle speech. Yet one remembers 1952 largely for Governor Thomas E. Dewey's countless speeches characterizing President Truman as a common thief; for Richard M. Nixon's half-hour display, on national television, of unbounded self-righteousness and self-pity; and of Senator Joseph R. McCarthy's outrageous attack, also before a national audience, on the character of Adlai E. Stevenson. The 1964 campaign has been almost unrelievedly offensive, but it never quite reached such depths as these.

Save for the fact that it got under way in early summer and is now reaching a welcome end, the campaign can scarcely be said to have had a history. No new issues emerged, no old ones were ever joined. It was, as it generally is when an incumbent runs, the challenger who established the tone. "The answers to America's problems are simple," Senator Goldwater said in an early speech. Certainly the answers Goldwater proposed were

165

breathtaking in their simplicity—a "win" strategy in the Cold War, a "free" economy, and, day after melancholy day, "morality." On occasion, Johnson said that the problems themselves were complex and thus would not yield to simple solutions, but beyond that he rarely discussed the problems, and his own answers were, in large part, one-word incantations—"peace," "responsibility," "compassion." Inanity bred inanity. The President found himself bellowing to the electorate that "the world you save [from Goldwater, by voting for Johnson] may be your own." The horror in this seemingly maniacal plea was that it seemed to contain a large, coarse grain of truth. No one thought President Johnson a plausible messiah, but a good many thought that Goldwater's "win" strategy could lead to disaster.

Toward the close of the President's campaign, there was a slight change in his style. He moved from a defense of past Democratic administrations to evangelistic and almost utopian visions of the future, which he sometimes delivered in language appropriate to the pulpit, as in Pittsburgh on October 27:

So here's the Great Society. It's the time—and it's going to be soon—when nobody in this country is poor. It's the time—and there's no point in waiting—when every boy or girl can have all the education that boy or girl can put to good use. It's the time when there is a job for everybody who wants to work. It's the time when every slum is gone from every city in America, and America is beautiful. It's the time when man gains full domination under God over his own destiny. It's the time of peace on earth and good will among men.

To say that the "issues" were never discussed is merely to say that the expected occurred. It is not, though, to say that it was a campaign barren of issues. On the contrary, it was uncommonly rich in them. Nearly all of them were embodied in the person of the Republican candidate. Barry Goldwater is himself one large bundle of issues, and when we know how the country has responded to him we will know a good deal more of who we are and what we are. Another way of putting it is to say that the "choice" he offered was, first, between the kind of American community we are today and a community of a radically different sort, and, second, between preserving the peace by means of institutional reform and diplomatic accommodation, on the one hand, and, on the other, by seeking diplomatic "victory" by ultimatum. Goldwater's domestic politics are pre-industrial. He seems never to have heard of the division of labor. He looks with disfavor on the doctrine that national governments in industrial societies must assume responsibility for keeping the strains and dislocations that industrialism brings within tolerable limits. And his view of foreign policy is pre-atomic. He acknowledges no fundamental changes in the realities of power since 1945—or for that matter since 1900. It is his view, advanced almost daily in his campaign, that this country can get what it wants on any continent merely by confronting its adversaries with a threat to use its power. He is confident that by this means "Communism"—which he thinks of in purely ideological terms—can be destroyed as a force in world affairs.

The debate, such as it has been, was conducted in invective, in angry slogans, and in coded platitudes. Yet the electorate appears to have attended it with remarkable sophistication. And in this there is something of a mystery, since there was never really anything that presented itself as fit for consideration by the discriminating intelligence. The campaign of 1960 was hardly more stimulating than this one, but at least there were the televised debates, which afforded opportunities to take the measure of the men and of their minds. At the Presidential level this year, there was nothing of the sort. And in fact, television has played little part in the campaign. It was said that Senator Goldwater would rely heavily on it toward the end, but he never did, perhaps because his early experiences of it were unrewarding. He found it hard to attract an audience. Johnson made one major appearance—to discuss, on October 18, the change of leadership in the Soviet Union and the United Kingdom and the nuclear detonation in China—and he did, as President, command an audience. Though of course the speech was "political"—as anything said close to an election necessarily is—there is no evidence that it was in any sense important to his campaign. Paradoxically, it was a turning point of sorts in the Goldwater campaign. Dean Burch, the Republican National Chairman, asked the Federal Communications Commission to direct the networks to give the Republicans equal time. The FCC declined to do this, but one network gave Burch himself fifteen minutes to give the party's "answer" to Johnson. To the astonishment of the network, Burch used much of the time to appeal for money. The appeal, it was said, was enormously successful. A debt-ridden committee was suddenly debt-free and has in prospect a surplus. The Presidential campaign has been notable for the fact that no one but the principals played a significant part in it. The political technicians were seldom seen and seldom, one gathers, occupied with matters of much gravity. Neither candidate has had a Mark Hanna or a James A. Farley. Dean Burch, the Republican National Chairman, was, it appears, busier purging and reorganizing the Republican National Committee than directing the Republican campaign. (An early step in reorganization was the removal, on orders of Burch's deputy, John Grenier, of Alabama, from headquarters walls of all pictures of Abraham Lincoln and Dwight D. Eisenhower.) President Johnson was his own campaign manager; John Bailey, of Connecticut, who moved in as Democratic National Chairman upon the nomination of John F. Kennedy in 1960, remained on the job but was seldom heard as a party spokesman. Nor did the elder statesmen of either party do much for the candidates. General Eisenhower several times affirmed his intention of working for Goldwater, but he did, so far as can be learned, no work at all in the early part of the campaign. Close to the end, he was hospitalized—providentially, he may have felt—with an affliction that affected his vocal cords. Herbert Hoover was on his deathbed through most of the campaign and expired on October 20. Harry Truman vigorously endorsed President Johnson's candidacy—at one point he told the President that he regarded Democratic victory in the 1964 election as more important than his own victory in 1948—but he, too, was in indifferent health and was, like Eisenhower, hospitalized in October.

The campaign has been too serious and too bitter to be relieved by the atmosphere of carnival and sport that have so often been part of American politics. There was no campaign music of note. "Hello, Lyndon," borrowed from the Broadway musical "Hello, Dolly," was a pleasant enough tune, but it turned out not to wear very well. "The Battle Hymn of the Republic" has been much heard at Goldwater rallies—where Confederate flags have often been seen and denunciations of the Civil Rights Act frequently heard. On the Republican side, the partisans were angry, joyless, urgent, and, as such people generally are, full of a sense of beleaguerment. On the Democratic side, the atmosphere has been somewhat more festive because the partisans have had somewhat more reason for confidence. But the Democratic campaigners, too, were urgent men and, much of the time, bitter ones. Though they were confident of victory, what they sought was more than victory. Their end was not merely to retire Senator Goldwater, but to destroy the movement he led.

History is made by men who are cast in the role of leadership. The conservative push in America cannot be politically focussed without a leader who can bring together the South, the Midwest, the Mountain States, New England, and the Pacific Northwest. For the first time since the death of Robert A. Taft, such a leader exists. He is, inescapably, Senator Barry Goldwater. Where Taft was a rock, Goldwater is the flint and steel which can strike fire in the electorate.

—Ralph de Toledano, in *The Winning Side: The Case for Goldwater*, a memorable book and one that is hereby commended to those eager to revisit 1963 and 1964. There are two editions. A hard-bound one, suitable for permanent collections, was issued by G. P. Putnam at $3.95, and a paperback was issued by the MacFadden-Bartell Corporation at 60 cents. The texts are the same except that here and there in the second "Johnson" replaces "Kennedy." I'd suggest getting the first edition and making one's own revisions. Many friends will wish to savor it, and my paperback has barely survived three readings. Also, the Putnam, or collector's, edition has endorsements by Senator John Tower and William F. Buckley, Jr. They admired the book immensely, and so, I think, will you.

We are convinced that the nomination of Barry Goldwater will result in substantial increases in Republican membership in both houses of Congress.

—Manifesto issued by fifty-four Republican Representatives on June 19, 1964. Twenty-one of the seats the signers held went to Democrats on November 3.

* WHY NOT VICTORY? A LETTER
FROM WASHINGTON

November 8, 1964

Back in the early summer, when it was becoming apparent that moderation was a virtue that would go unrewarded at the Republican National Convention, some politician here said that Barry Goldwater and Lyndon Johnson were leading us into a new political order—a one-and-a-half-party system. This seems to have been as accurate a forecast as any ever made by Gallup, Harris, Roper, Lubell, CBS, or Nostradamus. By most of the accepted standards, the Republican Party today is to the Democratic Party as one is to two. There are now, and will be next year, two Democratic governors for every Republican governor. In the Senate, when it meets in January, the ratio will be the same. In the House, it will be slightly more favorable to the Democrats, who will outnumber the Republicans two to one and will have about fifteen spare votes, which may come in handy when the weather is bad or the golfing is good. Taking the state legislatures as a whole, it seems that there will be just about two Democrats for every Republican. And only this morning, Dr. Gallup announced that there are now two Americans who regard themselves as Democrats for every one who regards himself as a Republican—or, to be a bit more precise, fifty-three Democrats for every twenty-five Republicans. (The trend, he says, has run steadily against the Republicans ever since 1940, when there were thirty-eight Republicans for every forty-two Democrats.) In a way, these figures seem to call for a reading of the Presidential returns rather different from the one that most people here have been disseminating. Dr. Gallup's findings suggest that it was not the Democratic candidate but the Republican one who ran stronger than his party. In the popular vote, the Johnson total fell about four million, or five percentage points, short of being double the Goldwater total. It was a peculiar campaign, to say the least, and both candidates got votes that could hardly be counted as expressions of confidence in the parties they represented. But it seems a fact beyond dispute that it was Goldwater who made the largest single raid on the opposition. For among his twenty-six million votes was a bloc of six million from the Old Confederacy, with the largest clusters coming, according to the tallies now being made, from out where the clay is red and the woods are piney and the yeomanry is about as Republican, or "conservative," as Cotton Ed Smith, Pitchfork Ben Tillman, or Ma and Pa Ferguson. Goldwater would have got these votes if his name had turned up on the Democratic ticket, the Dixiecrat ticket, or a lottery ticket. And if, four years hence, William Scranton, George Romney, and John Lindsay succeed in loading the Republican platform with favorable mentions of Abraham Lincoln, these voters will be found regrouped behind George Wallace, Orval Faubus, or—perhaps more likely—Lyndon Johnson, who is no doubt distressed by his poor showing in the popular vote and is probably already at work on plans to resolidify the South.

Raw statistics tend on the whole to conceal the true magnitude of the Republican disaster. They do not measure the echoing curses or the spattering of blood or the actual decline in power. The loss of thirty-nine seats in the House, for example, cannot be seen as a mere decline of representation by some 21 per cent. It is a descent from power of a quite substantial sort to something approaching total impotence. The Republican Party no longer has anything of value to contribute to the "conservative coalition." Even in the last days of the Eighty-eighth Congress, there was enough strength in the coalition to deny the President many things he wanted; just before adjournment, it beat back the medicare and Appalachia programs. Under Goldwater's leadership, the coalition has been wrecked. He has cleared the ground for a rampant liberalism*—there may even be the danger, for the President, that he will be given everything he asks for in larger quantities than he desires. Republican losses are augmented by Republican gains. The seven Republicans who rode Goldwater's coattails through the Alabama, Mississippi, and Georgia pea patches are liabilities. "Thank God for Goldwater," one of them said in every speech, and although they ran, as he did, on the Republican Party ticket, what they represent is the Goldwater party, whose interests had been quite adequately served by the Democrats they replaced. The Southern Republicans in the House can be relied upon, as can J. Strom Thurmond in the Senate, to resist and embarrass any efforts to rebuild the party in other sections.

It may turn out, though, that the losses in Congress are of trifling importance alongside those in the state legislatures. The computers are still groaning as they seek to digest these figures; the losses are, in any case, enormous, Democratic representation is up almost everywhere, and in a number of states, such as Indiana and Iowa, where Providence was believed to have ordained Republican dominance, the Democrats are in firm and no doubt unexpected control. This has happened at what is, from the Republican point of view, the worst imaginable time. If, four years ago, John F. Kennedy had got a much larger vote than he did and had led Democrats to power in normally Republican states, it would have seemed a lamentable development but scarcely a fatal one. State legislatures are a haven for deserving mediocrities and more than a few outright thieves, but their authority has been in decline throughout most of this century— a tendency Goldwater hoped to reverse—and if a party loses a few seats or even its majority standing, it can, if its power is firmly based, expect to recoup its losses when things get back to normal. But 1964 just happens to be no year for a cool

* "Modern liberalism is only a form of rigor mortis." Goldwater, speaking in Ralph de Toledano's *The Winning Side*.

acceptance of defeat in the state houses. It is the year in which the United States Supreme Court ruled, in *Reynolds* v. *Sims,* that the legislative districts in every state must be apportioned strictly on the basis of population and in such a way as to ensure that no man's vote gives him substantially more or less representation than any other man's vote. In most states, reapportionment is either already under way or scheduled to be begun by legislatures meeting next year. It was always clear that reapportionment could not fail to strengthen the Democrats even when it was undertaken by the Republicans, for it has been mainly the centers of Democratic power, the cities, that have been underrepresented. Most Republicans, though, have felt that if they could do the reapportioning themselves, they could find ways of lessening the damage it would do to the party's fortunes. But now in many state capitols where Democrats have been as negligible a minority as Buddhists, they are about to take charge of remapping all the political territory. It is doubtful whether anything else that happens in this decade will have so great an impact on American political life as the fulfillment of this court order, and the candidacy of Barry Goldwater has greatly diminished the role his party will play in it.

In the aftermath of the San Francisco convention, the Republicans who could see what was coming this year differed considerably in their estimates of how long it would take to reconstitute the party that came so close to victory in 1960. Some thought it could be done in the next four years; others thought it would take a generation, or roughly a quarter of a century. Now there are a few who think it can never be done, and not very many who think they will have more than half a party by 1968. The problem, as most people now see it, is not in getting rid of Dean Burch or the Goldwaterites on the national and state committees. The national committee of a party out of power is a feeble instrument—"an organization chart, not an army," as it has been put by that connoisseur of defeat Richard M. Nixon—and if its leadership can't be changed, it can be ignored and bypassed. Indeed, only a few weeks ago, when it

"EUREKA! WE CAME OUT AHEAD!"

"For the first time in memory, we finished in the black."
—Goldwater, November 6, 1964

was believed that the Goldwater campaign would end with an immense debt, the feeling in many Republican circles was that Burch should not be allowed to resign until he and his associates had settled everything with the creditors. The belief was a mistaken one; there turns out to be a surplus of some one and a quarter million dollars, and this, understandably, has contributed to an increase in the sense of urgency among those demanding Burch's resignation. But whether he stays or goes is not a matter of great political importance. The congressional leaders will speak for the party, and if the national committee is a nuisance to them they can set up some sort of parallel organization. The state committees are a lot more important, and the extent to which the Goldwater zealots have dominated them has been hugely exaggerated. Their strength has been mainly in the South, where his men have a tight grip on just about all the party machinery, and in the West. Their power comes to very little in any of the large industrial states—including California, where they made a desperate bid for control but failed to win it.

If health could be restored merely by stripping the Goldwater people of the offices they hold in the party, the work could be accomplished within the next two or three years. It is, however, not the officers but the troops that cause the greatest concern among the survivors here. The dilemma, as they see it, is that the Party cannot, on the one hand, afford continuing Goldwater leadership and cannot, on the other, afford to lose the Goldwater following. Ever since the spring primaries, it has been reasonably clear that all the talk about the "silent vote"—the "conservatives" who had been in political hideouts since 1932—was nonsense, and the election has proved it.* But there is a minority, anything but silent, that ceaselessly clamors for the kind of leadership Goldwater has given. By most appraisals, it amounts, at best, to about 20 per cent of the electorate, which, if it is assumed that it came out in full force for Goldwater, means

* Goldwater, in *U. S. News & World Report,* December 21, 1964: "I still believe that 'conservatism' attracts more than fifty percent of our people."

that it accounted for about fifteen million Republican votes this year, or for more than half the Goldwater total. A party that is only half a party faces some appalling problems if it has to begin rebuilding by alienating half its present supporters and becoming, then, a quarter of a party. Yet this is the prospect if Goldwater and Goldwaterism are not to be repudiated and reviled. Indeed, it rather misses the point even to speak of these people as "supporters" of Republicanism or as capable of being "alienated." To them—as to their leader in 1964—doctrinal rectitude is vastly more important than the spoils of party victory. This has always been true of them (it is true, too, of many groups within the Democratic coalition, *e.g.,* organized labor, the intellectuals, leaders of the Negro resistance), but the truth was one that had less meaning in the days before the Eastern leaders revealed their vulnerability. Landon, Willkie, Dewey, Eisenhower, and Nixon could get the votes of the radical right without making a conspicuous play for them because the radical right—outside the South, at least—could never support the Democrats and because, further, it had no reason to think it could ever be master in the Republican house. There was plenty of muttering about the need for "a choice, not an echo," but in most sections the Republican echo was preferred to the choice the Democrats offered.

Now, though, the Goldwater campaign is part of Republican history—a glorious part, one can be sure, in the rightist view— and it is hard to believe that those Scots who have with Goldwater marched and bled will ever line up behind the likes of George Romney or William Scranton, who, as Goldwater himself has said, did far more damage to the crusade of 1964 than any Democrat did. To say this is not to detract from Lyndon Johnson's performance. But the Goldwater the President chose to run against was the Goldwater of the portraits first painted by Rockefeller, Lodge, Scranton, and other "Eastern Establishment" figures whom the rightists quite properly identify as the enemy within the gates. The Easterners would like to unload the Goldwater zealots, and success in this enterprise would doubtless make it easier for a Republican candidate from somewhere near the center to win back Maine and Vermont and possibly even Ohio and Illinois. But in a great many parts of the country it would be as hard on the party to lose them as it has been to win them. Organizations like the Conservative Party in New York would spring up all over the place and further complicate Republican problems. The need then would be to build on a base of the ten or eleven million voters who accepted the Goldwater "choice" but could be counted upon to accept an "echo," too. Assuming that it was possible for the party to hold on to at least a part of the Goldwater legions—say a third, or between four and five million—there would still be a shortage of close to twenty million votes. It seems quite a shortage to make up even in a quarter of a century—especially by a party that, according to Dr. Gallup, has lost a third of its following over the past quarter of a century.

The electorate performed as the polling agencies had predicted it would. The opinion samplers were astonishingly accurate not only about the national division but, in nearly every instance, about the regional, economic, and ethnic variations. "Farley's law," which states that an insignificant number of voters change their minds between Labor Day and Election Day, appears to have been confirmed. And, in the light of this year's experience, it might well be revised to cover the entire period between the naming of the candidates and Election Day. Goldwater never gained or lost much after San Francisco. In this city, though, there are a lot of people who retain vivid memories of the summer and fall of 1948, when the principal topics of conversation were how many electoral votes Thomas E. Dewey would win by and what sort of Cabinet appointments he might make, and while this year's campaign lasted, there were very few who had enough confidence in the polls to dismiss altogether the possibility of a Goldwater victory. It was a possibility that caused uneasiness even among many who would welcome an administration well to the right of the present one. For a Goldwater government would have been, by political design and by ideological definition, a minority government. In the first place, it could have come into being only by exploiting the inequities and quirks of our political and social systems. The basis of the "Southern strategy" was to begin building an electoral plurality with the hundred and twenty-eight votes of eleven states, in nearly all of which a huge and aggrieved mass of citizens remains largely disfranchised. To these votes were to be added, first, those of the Mountain States which have more representation in the Electoral College than they would be entitled to if population were the determining factor, and, second, the votes of a few large industrial states in which—so the strategists thought—fear and hatred of Negroes were running strong enough among many other minorities to produce votes for Goldwater. Thus, even if Goldwater had managed to win a simple majority of both popular and electoral votes, he would nevertheless have been a minority President—one who owed his victory to disfranchisement and one, moreover, who fully intended to pursue policies that only minorities had ever endorsed.

To envision a Goldwater government in 1965 was, for most people here, to foresee at once a deep crisis in international relations and a Constitutional crisis of great severity and inherent insolubility. It was to envision a government that might very well find itself unable to govern and, at the same time, unable by any legal means to be relieved of the responsibility of governing. The shape of the international crisis was difficult to imagine. A great deal might have depended on what Goldwater said and did in the first few hours and days after victory. He would, in any event, have had to say a good deal to keep a single ally. It is doubtful if there is a government anywhere in the world—with the possible exception of the one that up to last night was hanging on to power in South Vietnam—that would have wished to be associated with Goldwater's ultimatum diplomacy. One almost certain development, it was thought, would have been an announcement by the Soviet Union that it was taking advantage of the escape clause in the Treaty of Moscow that enables a signatory power to withdraw on three months' notice. And the outgoing President Johnson would doubtless have had to follow suit. (On "Meet the Press" on January 5, Goldwater was asked, "If you were President and you were able to renounce the treaty, you would do it?" He replied: "If it appeared to be to our advantage to test in the atmosphere, yes, I would do it." In the debates over the treaty, he had several times said that atmospheric tests *were* to our advantage.) It was by no means difficult to imagine the outlines of the Constitutional crisis. Not even the most confident of Goldwater's supporters ever thought he had a prayer of getting a Congress sympathetic to his proposals. In the Senate, a Republican majority was a mathematical impossibility. In the House, a Republican majority was at least conceivable, but a Goldwater majority was not, particularly since Republican candidates by the dozen had been hostile to his nomination and his candidacy. He would have experienced difficulties unprecedented in American history in even as elementary a matter as getting Senate confirmation of his Cabinet appointments. And congressional resistance would have been accompanied by resistance within his own branch of the government. Every modern President—and especially those who propose change and reorganization—has had many hopes dashed by bureaucratic resistance within the government departments that are supposedly under Presidential direction. The resistance to Goldwater would have been massive and, perhaps quite literally, overwhelming. It was quite impossible for most people here to envision the Department of State implementing Goldwater's foreign policy; if he were intent on implementation, he would have to construct an entirely new agency. And despite his insistence that he would be committed by his oath of office to enforce the Civil Rights Act of 1964, his election, made possible by Southern support, would have been read in the South as a license to disregard the act in its entirety. He had never retreated from the view that two of its most important provisions were unconstitutional, and toward the close of the campaign he took to denouncing the whole idea of legal defenses against segregation and discrimination. His election would have bred defiance throughout the South and in much of the North, and would have forced Negroes everywhere to conclude that there was, and for a long time would be, no hope for a redress of their grievances in law or in politics. In such circumstances, a spreading violence would have been as predictable as the sunset.

It is doubtful if any one man in our history has ever attracted as much institutional censure as Goldwater, and as little institutional support. He ran without the endorsement or encouragement of any recognized power bloc or special interest, with the exceptions—if they can be counted in that category—of the rightist propaganda organizations, certain oil and cattle interests in the Southwest, and certain military lobbies. Against him were ranged the most influential sections of the press, all of organized labor, most of organized religion, a considerable part of the business community, all but a handful of the intellectual and educational communities, most farm organizations, Negro groups without exception, and other ethnic organizations almost without exception. If, in the face of this, he had managed to patch together a coalition of the politically discontented and dispossessed that could win him the Presidency, he would have been a President without a power base of any sort. No doubt the more responsible leaders of the institutions that opposed him would have come together in an attempt to reach some kind of accommodation with him to keep the country from tearing itself to pieces. Even so, we would still have had four years of unresolved crisis, for our Constitution provides no means of resolution except in quadrennial elections. If Goldwater and the world had allowed us to withdraw from the world for a time, we could probably have weathered it out. But it would have been far from a sure thing.

Anybody who tries to guess now what the party will do in 1968 has to be an idiot.

—Goldwater, press conference, Montego Bay, Jamaica, November 14, 1964

✳ **In your heart, you know he's right.**
— Goldwater campaign slogan

✳ **The American people, unfortunately, vote too much from the heart and not enough from the head.**— Goldwater, in a postelection interview, *U. S. News & World Report,* December 21, 1964

✳ **Anybody who tries to guess now what the party will do in 1968 has to be an idiot.**— Goldwater, in a press conference at Montego Bay, Jamaica, November 14, 1964

✳ **One of the reasons I chose Bill Miller is that he drives Johnson nuts.** —Goldwater, as quoted in James A. Perry's *Barry Goldwater,* Dow Jones Company, 1964

✳ **"[In] the meantime, if they [other people] have to have a dictator in order to keep communism out, then I don't think we can object to that."** — Goldwater, in an interview with John Rolfson on "Issues and Answers," ABC-TV, April 7, 1963

✳ **"I would turn to my Joint Chiefs of Staff and say, 'Fellows, we made the decision to win, now it's your problem.'"** — Goldwater, in *Der Spiegel,* June 30, 1964

✳ **"One Eisenhower in a generation is enough."**— Goldwater, in response to an inquiry about the Presidential capabilities of Milton Eisenhower, as quoted in *Time,* July 24, 1964

 "I hope Tshombe beats the hell out of the United Nations." — Goldwater, as quoted in *Barry Goldwater: Portrait of an Arizonan* by Edwin McDowell, Regnery, 1964, p. 240